AMONG
THE LIVING
AND
THE DEAD

AMONG THE LIVING AND THE DEAD

A TALE OF EXILE
AND HOMECOMING
ON THE WAR ROADS
OF EUROPE

INARA VERZEMNIEKS

W. W. NORTON & COMPANY

INDEPENDENT PUBLISHERS SINCE 1923 ♦ NEW YORK ♦ LONDON

For information about permission to reproduce selections from this book,
write to Permissions, W. W. Norton & Company, Inc.,
500 Fifth Avenue, New York, NY 10110

For information about special discounts for bulk purchases, please contact
W. W. Norton Special Sales at specialsales@wwnorton.com or 800-233-4830

Manufacturing by Berryville Graphics
Book design by Brooke Koven
Production manager: Julia Druskin

ISBN 978-0-393-24511-0

W. W. Norton & Company, Inc.
500 Fifth Avenue, New York, N.Y. 10110
www.wwnorton.com

W. W. Norton & Company Ltd.
15 Carlisle Street, London W1D 3BS

1 2 3 4 5 6 7 8 9 0

To Livija,
who helped me build a home from what was lost.
And to Ausma,
who waited for me there.

What is told here has happened,
although I tell it in my style and manner.

—EDUARDO GALEANO

I looked to the sky and to the ground and straight ahead
and since then I have been writing a long letter to the dead
on a typewriter that has no ribbon, just a thread of horizon
so the words knock in vain and nothing sticks.

—TOMAS TRANSTROMER, *Baltics*

I am wandering, lost
In my father's fields:
Where I left a meadow
I found a birch grove.

—FROM THE LATVIAN FOLK SONGS/TONE POEMS
KNOWN AS THE DAINAS

AMONG
THE LIVING
AND
THE DEAD

I

THE ROAD I must travel to reach my grandmother's lost village is like tracing the progression of an equation designed to restore lost time. Each kilometer that carries me from Riga seems to subtract five years.

First there are the gas stations and Swedish supermarket chains, signs ever burning. Next come the old Soviet-era apartment buildings, stubborn blocks of concrete and pebble-dash, their facades brittle and peeling like the skin of old wasps' nests. Down in the parking lots, old women pile bones for the stray cats.

From this point, the land begins its reclaiming, grass and Queen Anne's lace rooting through abandoned concrete slabs. Occasionally, a house will appear, canted and suffering, maybe with a slope-shouldered figure poking at a smoldering brush pile in the yard. But just as quickly, these glimpses are smothered by the trees.

Sometimes a house stands still long enough to admit that it is abandoned, portions of the roof skinned away to reveal blackberries growing on the inside, the surrounding fields neck-high and riotous.

Soon the village center announces itself: first come the thumps of the railroad tracks and then the houses, clad in wood worn as gray as lichen. Sheets snap on clotheslines. A van parked in a gravel turnout advertises smoked carp. A man teeters along the shoulder on a child's bicycle, a bottle wrapped in brown paper poking its neck from his jacket pocket.

The center holds for a few more seconds and then abruptly, it gives up and lets the fields resume their patter: rapeseed, rye, rapeseed, rye.

Eventually, the fields stop just long enough to take a breath, revealing a long rutted driveway.

At the end sits a home made from brick, modern by the standards of the countryside, clearly built within the last sixty years, after the Second World War, though the sun and the snow and the rain have worried it to the point of exhaustion.

The yard is still, except for three chickens, muttering and picking their way across tindered grass. The house acts as if it is empty, though I know someone is inside, waiting for me.

I sit for a moment, listening to the car's cooling engine, the chickens clapping their beaks, skimming the air for insects I can't see.

And just as I am trying to think of what I want to say—how to introduce myself to someone I have always and never known—the door to the little house opens, and I see my grandmother.

Of course, by this time, my grandmother, the woman who raised me, has been dead for more than five years.

II

THIS IS why I had journeyed to my grandmother's lost village, nestled at the edge of Latvia, which is itself nestled at the edge of Europe's psychic north, south, east and west, or, as Pope Innocent III described it in a papal bull written in the thirteenth century, *the edge of the known world:*

Because I imagined, maybe, I might find her again in the old stories that still existed there.

Maybe what I mean to say is that I hoped to see, as the writer Rebecca West has put it, *what history meant in flesh and blood.*

And I suppose you could say this same recycled hope is what then moved me to return year after year, for what would ultimately become five consecutive years—until I could almost convince myself that I knew what it was like to live there, at the edge of the known world, as if I were an old story, too—at least for as long as the handful of weeks or months I managed to string together with each trip.

People say, *If the old stories are to be trusted,* when in fact the old stories never stopped being trusted, because trust is different than belief.

Belief is to faith, to truth, as trust is to comfort, to consolation.

Whether a matter of comfort, or of consolation, it's long been assumed of this region, where my grandmother was born, and where she made her life until the outbreak of the Second World War, that at some point each year the dead will come home.

And while general consensus holds that the dead's arrival can be read in the last stalks of grain, as they lengthen with the shadows, a signal that the fields are ready for the final pass of the scythe, no one can say which route the dead take on their annual pilgrimage, whether they walk alone or in procession. Now that I know my grandmother's lost village as well as I do, I like to imagine them cutting through its streets, lingering at the windows of the beauty salon where the last of the summer brides are having their hair set, slipping just past the reach of the angry goat tethered in the field adjacent to the crumbling apartment blocks.

It's possible, of course, that the dead prefer to make their way through the forests, where they can wander the nettle-hemmed paths looking for the last of the mushrooms, blackening now, the soft, gilled undersides thick with worms. Perhaps some of them recall where the woods hide the old Soviet missile base, birch trees growing from the roofs of the abandoned living quarters, piles of sodden clothing strewn at the entrances to the former command center, the deep furrows in the earth that mark the old beds of the nuclear warheads.

Should the dead choose to go through the fields, and it's evening, they can always fall in behind the line of heavily uddered cows, nipples shuddering and arcing milk with each thudden step. *Majamajamaja*, the herders sing and clap the air at their backs: *Homehomehome.*

Whether it is their childhood home or the last home that

the dead inhabited that they choose to visit during this time, no one really knows. But it's long been understood that once a year it is possible for the dead to suspend their exile from our world and cross back over to see how life has continued in their absence.

At one time, this idea would have been a source of great consolation to both the living and the dead, the possibility of return, however brief: to shoulder open the front door and find the row of boots, mud- and manure-crusted, still next to the far wall; one of the barn cats, broken-whiskered and notch-eared, secret sprayers of the phlox and hosta beds, trying to slink in behind them; and everyone around the table, stabbing cabbage around their plates, slathering black bread with butter. With each visit the dead would watch the lives of the not-dead progress: the new, fumbling couples, whispering and biting at down pillows; the blinking infants, swaddled and mewling; the graying heads, rasping and hacking into the closing dark.

And while the living wouldn't have seen the dead during this time, they understood that the dead were close, watching. They might have called out their names, talked to them, told them what they had missed over the past year, even set them a regular place at the table to encourage their company. But eventually, the living would decide that the visit had gone on long enough. Maybe they worried the dead were getting too comfortable, and might never want to leave. So they would politely inform the dead that it was time for them to go back to their world and wait until the next turn of autumn. They fell into an easy rhythm, the living and the dead, anticipating this annual reunion. And that was the first mistake: assuming that this was how things would be for eternity.

Because let's say suddenly, one year, the dead pushed open

the door to their old home and found everyone gone. Only empty rooms and overturned chairs and scattered papers, and a pile of white fur and bones in the old root cellar. It's hard to imagine the dead who found this would have wanted to linger for long, but because it was so new to them, this emptiness, maybe the dead liked having their old home to themselves at first, liked the way it allowed them to remember, unchallenged, the way things were in their time. But how many times can you unhasp all the safety pins in the sewing basket or place your palms on the surface of every mirror before you long for the presence of someone else to remind you that you were there, even in death.

So, when the dead returned again the next year and suddenly saw smoke clawing its way from the chimney, it's possible they felt something rising in them, too, something like hope. But once they crossed the threshold, they would see how everything was wrong: hay on the floors, ankle deep; the air thick with the smell of ammonia and dung; lowing from every room; scraping hooves; dozens of wet eyes meeting theirs in the dark; tails thumping against the walls of rooms turned stalls.

Even if it so happened that people eventually reclaimed the home of the dead from the cows, these newcomers would be no one the dead knew, or anyone who knew the dead—strangers speaking a strange language, living behind worn blankets that had been hung from the ceiling, crude dividers simulating some semblance of personal space, but that could not block out the sounds of the night, the groaning, the stiff shuffling to the back of the house, once a bedroom, now a makeshift privy, a hole hacked in the floor over which everyone squatted.

This is where, according to the logic of the living, it would have made sense to turn away, to retreat, maybe to the barn, empty except for the tractor that identified this as a collective farm, Russian-made, narrow-snouted, like the dogs that once slunk through here, long ago, secretly rooting through the stalls. But what do we, the living, know of how the dead define their losses.

What we can say is that a ritual the living had once imagined as a way for the dead to visit the homes of their memories had in fact become a search for a sign that these homes ever existed. Because after the blankets came down and the tractor disappeared from the barn, when trash and broken glass became the only records of habitation, then it was just fleas and mice and the occasional drunk curled up on the floor with a bottle, hiding from his wife in a place she would never think to look. And then after that: nothing. Only silence and decay, until all that remained was a jumble of broken boards in an overgrown field.

It was not just the physical home that had been lost to the dead: now no one sets a place for them anymore or anticipates their coming. In recent years, anyone who could be a descendant of the dead has left this countryside for more prosperous regions of Europe, places where it is possible to find not only work, but something that is certain to put more than a few hundred dollars in their pocket each month, and does not require one to muck stalls or buck hay or handle cows' teats.

The living might come back, briefly, for a wedding, or a christening, or a funeral, bottles clinking in plastic bags from the airport Duty Free. But the truth is that the dead now come more frequently than the not-dead; each year, after the harvest, if the stories can be trusted, stumbling through the forests, down the two-lane roads, across the shorn fields, searching for reassurance in a landscape that offers its reply in the form of empty clotheslines, untended graves, winter snows unbroken now by a single step.

THERE WAS A TIME when migrant flocks of Bewick's swans and whooper swans stopped here each year to winter in the bogs and fens. And so the region was named for these birds: Gulbene, from the Latvian word *gulbis* ("swan"). Located on the country's eastern edge, two hours from the Russian border, this place has witnessed centuries of migration and flight.

Some years it was members of the Order of the Brothers of the Sword who invaded, emissaries of the pope, their shields decorated with images of crucifixes and sharpened blades, their armor decorated with the spray of pagan blood. Other years, it was Ivan the Terrible's men, galloping through on horseback, rapiers drawn and torches in hand. Occasionally, there were Vikings, shaking snarled beards and shields, as well as soldiers who answered to a Swedish king who preferred to keep his facial hair in a trim Vandyke. Mostly though, it was armies dispatched by tsars and tsarinas, or those sent by kaisers. And after that, men who demanded that they be addressed as General Secretary of the Central Committee of the Communist Party. Or: Führer.

Once, the people who lived here didn't even bother distinguishing between the different routes that cut through their land. They simply called the paths in and out of the region by one name: war roads.

The roads through the region are mostly empty now—sometimes you can go hours without seeing another passing car—but there are days when it feels like the travelers of the war roads are out there still, all those ghost armies, advancing, retreating through the landscape, their presence suggested in the graffitied bunkers left to decay in the fields, and in the sudden disappearance of roadside trees, felled to block an incoming army's advance, and never replanted even all these decades later. They are always in the background, the sound of their phantom boots on the landscape as steady as a heartbeat: all these troops, from all these eras, a formation of tattered uniforms and missing limbs, marching through the collective memory, silently, endlessly—the harbingers of flight. And everyone in their path runs, is still running, through the years and generations.

This is where I come from, from this place of flight—daughter, granddaughter and great-granddaughter to those who once lived at the edge of the war roads, and who came to feel the roads' terrible pull. What happened to my family here happened long before I was born, but I know now that my life started the instant the road claimed them. That when it led them away from the land, all those years ago, and scattered them—some to the west, to be dropped at the edge of the ocean they called *silent* in their old language, and others to the east, to disappear into the territories of the banished—it made their exile mine, as much a part of me as any characteristic governed by heredity, like the nearsightedness that by the time I was seven would reduce my view of the world to what fell within an arm's length in front of me. Whatever lay in the distance, no matter how hard I tried to make out its contours, was always lost to me.

It helped that I was raised to believe in the existence of what I could not see. The language and stories of my childhood were always referencing hidden places. And one of those places waited on the other side of death. That's what the old homesick Latvians would say. That when we die, we go to live in a land that's found beyond the sun. They said this not as superstition or myth, but as habit, the reflexive tic of centuries of belief, now preserved in figures of speech that tended to emerge late at night, after the drinks had left everyone tremulous and heavy-lidded, such as *One day, we will meet in the place that exists beyond the sun.*

Beyond the sun, life is said to be not too dissimilar from this one. In fact, it's said that there, we do the same things we've always done, except we are no longer alive. Dead farmers look after dead cows that are herded by dead dogs. Dead children presumably go to schools where they are taught by dead teachers, who take their grading home at night to apartment buildings full of dead neighbors. Dead cats leave dead moles on the doorsteps of the dead.

There are moments when this strikes me as one of the most strange and beautiful ideas I have ever heard. And then there are moments when it makes me terribly sad, imagining a world unfolding parallel to this one where everyone is going through the motions of home, trying to hold on to its shape and memories. But it isn't home.

And now, from within this sadness, a realization: I'm not describing the dead anymore. I'm describing us, and our life in the little bowed house that we shared, my grandmother, Livija, my grandfather, Emils, and me.

I can still recall the way the house slunk low, like a person trying to hide; the plum tree that dropped its watery fruit on the front lawn in drifts, like snow; how the floor and the walls of the cellar beneath the house were only earth. And yet I hesitate to say that this is the place where I grew up. Maybe it is more accurate to say that this is the place where I learned of the existence of our true home, the one we could no longer see, but that called to us nonetheless from somewhere out there, far beyond the buzz of the paper mills; the single, ever-spewing spire of the copper smelter that turned the grass of the yards bordering it a mesmerizing yet unsettling chartreuse; and the stacks of shipping containers—corrugated blues and yellows and reds—that formed the edges of our accepted horizon.

Our true home, so the stories went, like the ones that my grandmother read to me at night from a battered edition of Grimms' fairy tales, the spine broken and held in place by tape, was far, far away, in the province of the swans, but we could never go back there again. Nor could anyone from that world visit us to remind us of who we were and where we came from, though once, my grandmother's mother had apparently shown up at our home, moments after her death, more than five thousand miles away, but only my grandmother saw her. She emerged from the seam that runs between darkness and daylight to stand at the edge of my grandmother's bed, as my grandfather snored and twitched beside her. It was the first time my grandmother had seen her mother in more than twenty years, and her face looked withered, like flowers left in a vase without water. My grandmother opened her mouth to say something, but before she could speak, before she could form the words *forgive me*, her mother leaned over and placed a callused palm on my grandmother's curlered head. She let it rest there for a moment. Then she disappeared.

My grandmother seemed to accept the brief terms of this visitation. She, too, as I understood it, had disappeared just as quickly from her family's life, though her vanishing had been the living kind, born of war and panic, the heavy trundle of red-starred tanks over cobblestone, airships swimming overhead, flames where roofs should have been, and from somewhere nearby the sound a building makes just before it crumbles: a whoosh of air, like a breath released from a cracked sternum.

Alone, with two small children—her husband away at the Russian front—my grandmother had monitored the climax of the Second World War from a rented apartment in the Latvian capital with an address of 71 Peace Street. Between the choiring of the bombs, she breast-fed her newborn son and hoped she could remain in one place long enough for her body to heal, for the bleeding to finish. But as the glass in the windows rippled, and it became clear she couldn't wait where she was any longer, she dropped diapers into a sack and tied a scarf around her shoulders.

She picked up her three-week-old son. Made her two-year-old daughter clasp her hand. And ran.

As she had explained it to me growing up, there was no time to write a letter, to address it to the family who waited three hours to the east in Gulbene, in the brown-shingled farmhouse where my grandmother had been born, and which she had left only a few years before, the first in her family to venture beyond its boundaries for a new life in the city. The day she left the farm, her whole family had accompanied her to the train station, still in their milking boots, and they had cried and waved at my grandmother until the train finally pulled beyond view. Now, there was no time for my grandmother to say good-bye to her mother and her father and her brother and her sister, no way to tell them where she was heading, because even she had no idea. It was too late for her to do anything, except to try to stay on her feet and ahead of the Russian troops, thousands of them, marching behind the battle standard of the USSR, red-silkscreened with hammer and sickle—Latvia's new flag.

I know now that my grandmother left Latvia at the beginning of October 1944. It was late June 1945 before she finally crossed into British-occupied territory in the north of Germany. There, she and her children were officially registered as Displaced Persons, ultimately assigned to a refugee camp on the outskirts of the port city of Hamburg, where she and the children sometimes went on day passes to pick through the firebombings' char, burned brick and pooled metals, searching for things to trade or that might fuel their cook-fires. But when she was alive, my grandmother never emphasized the length or the difficulty of her journey across Europe, what she might have seen in her memories that she wished she could forget. And while the stories she told implied great difficulty and sorrow, she erased them of the grim particulars, made them archetypal enough to feel memorable, recognizably powerful without exposing me to the specificity of her own traumas: *A friend from Riga joined me, to help with the children; we slept in the woods at night and dried diapers on branches; we looked for farmhouses and offered to help with the cows in exchange for milk, a place to sleep.* Her story existed for me only in simple outline, like the life-size self-portraits we made in elementary school art class by lying on our backs on a blank expanse of butcher paper, while the teacher traced our jittering bodies, our physical presence in the world suggested through negative space, the hollows held inside the lines. In much the same way, I accepted the presence of what went unspoken in my grandmother's war stories as evidence of something that did not have to be made explicit in order to be registered, understood. She did not have to say terror or shame or anguish for me to feel these things held inside her, as clearly as if I had held them inside me, too.

My grandmother, Livija, chose instead to speak about the place she had left, as if she had never left. Over the years—as she lay on her pallet in the refugee camp, where she would live so long after the war that she and my grandfather could trace the years by the additions to their family, two children becoming four, two boys and two girls; as she clutched the family's passports and entrance papers to the United States and felt the transport plane's rising, its wings tipped to the sea—my grandmother never stopped saying the name of the home she had lost.

T-a-c-o-m-a, she practiced, as the smell of the mills punched through the cracks in the windows of her new home, an apartment in a downtown tenement where the volunteers from Tacoma Lutheran Family Services had indicated through gentle pantomime that the family of six now lived. But that word always remained unsure on her tongue. It would never sound as natural as the way she said *Lembi*, which she had first learned from her grandfather, a shoemaker from Gulbene who eschewed whiskers but let his eyebrows grow like cumulus clouds. The name he had bestowed on the two-bedroom farmhouse he built under the shelter of two maple trees. There he raised his only child, a boy, who would grow up to become my grandmother's father, a man of waxed mustaches and a fine way with hops, known for the batches of ale he kept in the granary, always enough to lend to a wedding or a wake. My grandmother's mother was ten years younger than her husband, and everyone agreed that she possessed the patience required to ret the farm's flax and spin its fibers into linen so fine and soft that it felt weightless, yet she was also quick to snap a switch from the nearest tree if she sensed the slightest misbehavior.

This was the world my grandmother, Livija, was born into: where landscape was lineage, and the span of a life could be measured by all that was held within the farm's boundaries. There, she knew it was summer by the smell of fresh mown hay; fall when the saffron milk caps rose from the decay of the forest floor; spring by the storks winging overhead. Each day was organized around the rhythm and habits of the cows, and almost as soon as my grandmother and her siblings could walk, they were toddling barefoot behind the slow-hoofed cortege as it mouthed its way across the pastures, and they remained with the herd until evening, when it was time to drive them back to their places in the barn. The children did this for years, back and forth, stall to pasture, until they had spent more time in the company of cows than any other living being. Long after my grandmother had settled in America, she would visit the dairy barn at the state fair, wandering the labyrinthine complex and appraising each cow with tender eyes. Always, there would be a cow or two that stirred something close to rapture in her. Oh, how beautiful, she would say, standing unself-consciously in her heels among the splatters, taking care to address the animal directly. What a fine cow you will be.

My grandmother spent more than a decade not knowing what had happened to her family and to the farm after she fled Latvia. Even when she was finally able to reestablish contact with her relatives in Gulbene, communication was sporadic, halting, the letters subject to censors' eyes. How far away she felt from the days when she could sit with her family in the kitchen of the farmhouse, everyone nursing cups of hot tea, replaying the events of the day. Often, it was a catalog of nothing. Maybe a heifer had been born with a broken mouth. A cloud had passed overhead in the shape of a girl. The bees seemed agitated. Now, as she sat alone at her kitchen table in Tacoma, crying over the pages of the latest stilted letter— *We went far away to work for a time*—there was a part of my grandmother that understood she could never return to that place again. But there was also a part of my grandmother that refused to accept the idea that she could never return to that place again.

In the end, my grandmother decided to try to find a way to occupy the space that bordered both realities: until the day she could return to the farm, she would rebuild it here, in America, board by board, through memory.

At first she did it by herself, silently setting the survey lines. She raised the sky just far enough overhead so that it felt as if you could reach up and brush your fingers against it when you lay on your back in the grass. She smoothed the fields out to the edges of the horizon, and then summoned the forests, dense and dark. Behind the screening branches, she placed the anthills and the badger burrows. Reluctantly, she conjured the mosquitoes and horseflies, if only for the sake of accuracy, the way they blackened the summer air.

Orchard sown, she replanted the gooseberries and currants and let their rows grow unruly, vines curling back on themselves like the ends of her father's mustache. She staked the stems of the lolling dahlias and drove posts for the picket fence deep into the soil, but still it would list. She bucked hay into the loft, and stacked logs for winter's approach. But since this was a world summoned entirely from memory, there were places where the landscape dropped away without any explanation, sudden chasms of white space, unresolved constructions. The milking barn contained stools, but not a single churn. The horse grazed endlessly, reins dragging through clover. Inside the house, some of the rooms appeared never to have been framed or plastered; the same hallway led to different bedrooms each time it was accessed. Outside the kitchen window lilacs bloomed, regardless of the season.

LIKE A GHOST, my grandfather had simply shown up one day at the refugee camp where my grandmother was living following her flight from Latvia. My grandmother had spent the last two years fearing he was dead.

Number of family members? the camp intake forms had asked. *Four,* my grandmother had written, then scratched it out. Above it, she wrote much more faintly, *Three.*

My grandfather could not hide from her the hole where his eye had once been, but he refused to say anything about his time in the war. And no one ever asked, even though they knew that this was what made him rock in his chair for hours, his hands fluttering in his lap like birds with snapped wings, that this was what made him slam his fist down on the table even when there was no point to be made.

As a little girl, I learned to watch for the moments when my grandfather slipped away from us, knew, when the trembling started, that if I put a small hand on his arm and spoke his name, I could eventually make it stop. *You are here with me, Papa,* I would say, trying to call him back. And he would agree—*yes, yes, yes!*—but I could see by the set of his brow he was still someplace else. We lived quietly, my grandfather, grandmother and I, rarely venturing far beyond the house, except for my grandparents' nightly walk beneath the freeway underpass and down the dead-end street, past the trailer court and the overgrown field where my grandmother sometimes waded into the grass to pinch the heads off wild chamomile flowers that she then pocketed to dry. Two times a week, my grandfather chauffeured us into downtown Tacoma for choir practice and worship services with the other Latvian exiles, all of them drawn to this area by the sponsorship of the local Lutheran church. Few of them had known one another in their old country, but now war and coincidence had made them a community, albeit a small one. By the time I came to live with my grandparents, the number of congregants hovered around fifty, from an original three hundred members, though no one was quite sure how to count the woman who everyone suspected must be part Russian, given the suspicious way she made her *pirags*—with lard in the dough and boiled eggs and beef for filling: like swallowing stones, it was whispered.

Every Thursday and Saturday, we gathered in a rented church basement, where we sat on metal folding chairs that had been arranged in narrow rows. I tried not to stare at the man who had a hook for a hand, or to squirm when suddenly I was crushed against the breasts of a woman who always wept and whispered another girl's name as she embraced me. The pastor gave long and tremulous sermons in Latvian, and when I grew restless, my grandmother would let me flip through her hymnbook, really just a stack of mimeographs, handwritten scores reconstructed from the congregants' memories, the songs they carried with them when they fled. I was always the youngest person in attendance by at least sixty years; the congregants' own children—most of whom had been about my age when they first arrived here as refugees with their parents in the 1950s—were all grown now and deep into the work of making new lives in this new land, sometimes even calling themselves by new names, easier for American tongues to grasp.

So only the elderly remained, which meant we had cycled through all the weddings and christenings that there would be. Now it was only funerals. Standing at the graveside we dipped our hands into an old coffee can filled with sand that someone had managed to smuggle out of Communist Latvia, and we took turns scattering it over the coffins' lids. Then we moved to the heap of raw earth, already studded with shovels. At first, the local cemetery didn't know what to make of us, the way we insisted on filling the graves ourselves. Sometimes the cemetery still sent its own gravediggers, who watched from behind headstones a few feet away as the old mourners swung their shovel blades, sweating and straining against suits and skirts. But the extra help was never needed. According to our traditions, no one left until every trace of soil had been scraped back into the hole, every last clod of dirt tamped down.

We entrusted our dead to a single funeral home, a brick building reminiscent of the Parthenon but located in an area of Tacoma more typically favored by bail bondsmen and pawnshops. The location mattered less than the fact that its owners were unquestioning, accommodating, even eager to learn our traditions, if it meant we would bring more business their way. If they ever thought it strange that we mixed Lutheranism with old pagan ways, they never said a word. They just made sure to keep copies of the Bible translated into Latvian on hand, as well as plenty of caskets crafted from oak, the tree the ancients had considered most sacred.

The ground those caskets were lowered into was in a section of cemetery the Latvians had purchased so that we could always be together, undisturbed. I'd been shown once where my grandparents' places waited, two anonymous rectangles of grass otherwise surrounded by occupied graves, and I liked to test myself whenever we found ourselves at the cemetery to see whether I could find my way back to them without any help, as if practicing for the day when it would fall to me to stand at the edge of the holes into which my grandparents had disappeared, feeling the old songs in my mouth, the weight of the sand from the old coffee can in my hand, the grit that it left behind in the creases of my palms and on the cuffs of my coat. It was like a silent command running behind everything we did, but in the cemetery, among the ever-expanding drift of headstones, I could hear it more clearly: *watch, listen, remember.*

This was how I knew someone had died: my grandmother would pull her paring knife from the kitchen drawer and head out to her garden to cut calla lilies, carrying them to the funeral cupped in the hollow of her hand.

This is how she soothed me back to sleep when I woke crying: the same hollow of her hand cupped against my cheek.

I began living with my grandparents following the collapse of my parents' marriage, a bitter coming-undone that had left them both emotionally incapable of caring for me; in my mother's case, it was also a legal ruling, her parental rights clipped, like the car she once steered off the road in a haze of drink. Custody was awarded to my father—the infant my grandmother had delivered as the bombs rained down on Riga—but my father, for his part, was lost deep in his own anger and sorrow and silence. Five years home from Vietnam, and he remained as tightly locked inside himself as the day he returned. Just as his own father had done, a quarter of a century earlier.

My father's not-speaking was much quieter than my grandfather's, not so much a refusal as a ceding to a kind of paralysis. He went to work, he went to school, but he seemed somewhere else, somewhere far away. And so my grandparents made a place for me in their home while he tried to find his way back to himself.

Where once I had known only one word for *mother*, now there were two. My grandmother was the one who took me to the backyard and showed me how to find the sweetest raspberries, hidden in the shade of the leaves. She was the one who set me on a kitchen chair, draped an apron around my neck and let me sink my fists into the warmth of rising dough. She was the one who said my name over and over again until it sounded like a song, the one who took me in her lap and comforted me after I spent hours on the porch with my little blue suitcase waiting for the mother who promised but seldom came.

I am now raising little Inara, my grandmother wrote to the relatives back in Latvia, who by this time she had not seen in thirty years—letters I would not discover until I was nearly forty, and had begun to visit Latvia myself.

I have fallen deeply in love with her, as she has with me. She calls this her home. But at night sometimes she jumps up screaming: "I want my daddy. Where is my daddy?" I don't know why, but she has not called out for her mother. At times, Inara calls me mommy. We speak Latvian at home, and she understands everything. She is enthralled with books and I read aloud to her from titles meant for much older children—stories of Hansel and Gretel and Snow White.

Sometimes, she sits alone with piles of books and "reads" by herself. We have no neighbors with children she can play with, but maybe it's not so important yet—she turns just three in December. When she first came into my care, Inara was so terribly anxious; it's required real effort to bring the little child to this place of calm.

And two years later she wrote: *Inara's mother comes to get her for visits only now and again.*

What she did not share in her letters she instead documented in a small spiral notebook, which I would not see until years after her death.

Once, I returned from one of those rare weekend visits with a burn on my chin in the shape of a lit cigarette.

And a few months after that entry, she wrote again in the notebook:

Tonight, when Inara came back it was like she was in a trance. Her mother laid her on my bed, and her eyes were open, but there was no motion in her for a very long time.

For as long as she lived, my grandmother never spoke to me about my mother, about what she did or did not do, what had happened or not happened in my earliest years, that I would need to be taken from her. And I never asked, as if I agreed that this was something that should not be given voice.

In the region of Latvia where my grandmother was raised, there are people who believe even to this day that the right words spoken in the right combination are a way of resurrecting what has been lost. Or, as an old man once asked me: Did I know that there were times when words could become more than words?

It's true, he insisted. Words can become as real as anything we see with our eyes or feel with these hands. I saw a man put out a fire using only words, he said. The house was engulfed and they'd run out of water, but then the man arrived, and he walked in circles around the house, very calm, one way and then another, repeating something into the flames.

This was how my grandmother sounded when she spoke to me of her former home, the farm she had rebuilt from memory, like someone who believed that the structure of it could be protected, even saved, through her telling.

We might be standing at the edge of my grandparents' property, which abutted a city salvage yard, feeding scraps of paper to the burn barrel. Then the wind would start, rattling the leaves of the nearby birch, and in its chatter my grandmother would hear the voices of the trees she had once moved through each day. Do you hear it? she would ask, urging me to follow her deep into the black and white thickets of her memories. This is what it sounds like when they speak.

Or maybe one morning we would wake to snow, and as we looked out the window together, she would remake its falling with her words until it became the hip-high drifts that sucked at the hooves of the draft horse, now harnessed to a sleigh upon which my grandmother's family rode, their laps weighted with blankets and furs.

She led me to the nest in the grass where she hid with her little brother from her mother's calls; let me peer into the cradle of her baby sister, born when my grandmother was fourteen. She revealed to me the location of the chest in which she had concealed love letters from a boy she thought she would marry before my grandfather, and sometimes I suspected I could hear the drawer scraping open inside her, as if she were pulling out the letters to reread them.

Each time she showed me something, it filled in a new location on the map of the property I now carried within me, until I began to think I knew the way back on my own. But even when I tried to retrace our path faithfully, because I was following my memories of her memories, it was like one of those pictures I had once seen where you thought you were dealing with a single, static image, say, a tree in full leaf, but depending on which direction you tipped the frame, the composition was completely altered; now that same tree was little more than withered branches. Sometimes the dog that barked at my approach was black and white; other times he was white marked with black. Sometimes my great-grandmother appeared in the yard, bent over the stump that turned wet with hens' blood after the thwack of the axe upon their necks, or maybe she was stoking the wood-fired stove that I had been warned was so hot it would cause the flesh of a curious child's hand to slide off like the skin of a snake. Other times, I would find her in bed, wrapped in a wet tangle of sheets, my grandmother at her side, pressing a spoon against her mother's mouth, the same way my grandmother fed me when I was sick.

I knew her brother and sister were there, wandering the property, too. My grandmother had gone to great lengths to help me recognize them—his knees were always skinned and he liked to help with the bees; she was small and fast, like the kittens who lived under the barn and would not let you hold them in your hands—but I found that whenever I invited them to join me, there was nothing where their faces should have been, as if I were peering into the well on the property where my grandmother cautioned you should not play, because if you fell, you would never touch bottom.

———

I DON'T KNOW if she grew tired of waiting, or if she simply came to accept the idea that the Latvia she had called home could only ever be accessed in memory, but where once she and my grandfather sat at kitchen table pecking out letters to the editor of the local paper on an old Olympia typewriter, the keys spackled with Wite-Out, so that their demands for the end to Latvia's illegal occupation sometimes looked like demands for an end to Ltv's llegl occupton, they now sat at the same table quizzing each other on the elements of the U.S. Constitution, the names of the state's congressional delegation. They did this, even as the television in the other room, always on in the background, and always tuned to CNN, began to relay images of hammers bashing sections of the Berlin Wall, of more than a million protesters clasping hands to form a human chain stretching unbroken from Tallinn to Vilnius.

My grandmother was in her seventies when she finally became a naturalized citizen of the United States, forswearing that she would *renounce and abjure all allegiance and fidelity to any foreign prince, potentate, state, or sovereignty, of whom or which I have heretofore been a subject or citizen.* Not long after, Latvia declared its independence.

She did not hurry back, as some exiles did. Many went immediately, returning with applications for Latvian passports and suitcases full of jewelry fashioned from Latvian amber, the ancient resin of prehistoric trees entombed at the bottom of the Baltic Sea, *a marrow discharged by trees belonging to the pine,* as Pliny the Elder described it, once coveted by the Romans and said to bring its wearers strength; and bottles of Black

Balsam, Latvia's national liquor, a drink that tastes as if one is alternately tonguing the unfurled buds of trees, then their hot pitch. It's revered for its medicinal qualities, is said to have brought Catherine the Great back from the brink of death, though in truth it is demonstrably curative only in that the first sip scours almost pleasantly from throat to bowel.

Among other exiles, I sensed euphoria, a strident reclaiming—"Nyet Nyet Soviet" T-shirts and family portraits taken on the steps of the Freedom Monument in downtown Riga tucked into that year's Christmas cards. Yet my own family seemed hesitant by comparison.

What I know of my grandmother's homecoming: when she saw her siblings again, for the first time in nearly fifty years, she wept, and they wept, and then everyone started talking at once and didn't stop until dawn. Later, as everyone slept, my grandmother let herself out, and walked the fields and forests for hours, alone. One day, she asked to go clean the graves of her parents and grandparents. She rubbed moss off the headstones, picked fallen branches from the ground. She slipped flowers in vases. Then, as she backed away, she raked the dirt around the headstones, erasing all footprints, all signs that she had ever been there at all.

Looking back now, I am surprised at how little I asked my grandmother about that trip and how little she offered, as if together we had reached the unspoken decision that it would be my job to retain the remembered version of her old home— the re-created farm of her youth that she had gifted to me— rather than the contemporary version she had discovered on her return.

Not long after my grandparents' trip to Latvia, my grandfather's heart began to fail, and within five years he was dead.

Less than six months after we buried him—dipping our hands into the old coffee can, now filled with the soil of free Latvia—one of my grandmother's neighbors dropped by to see how she was faring. When the neighbor knocked but received no response, she put her eye to a gap in the crocheted hanging my grandmother had placed over the window in the front door. She spotted my grandmother's glasses first, resting in the pile of the rug, then the soles of my grandmother's slippered feet.

After the first stroke, I told myself that my grandmother would recover, that there would still be time for us to go back through her memories again. But a second, stronger stroke followed, and this time she disappeared into territory that I couldn't access.

Sometimes, when I went to visit her at the nursing home where she now lived, and if I happened to catch her in the half-conscious moments just following a nap, she might string together a few labored words, enough to tell me that she was spending time with those long lost to her, my grandfather, her parents, her brother, how they had been traveling together to all the places she had never been before, like Paris. Other times, she was back in the refugee camps; once, she told me she had been nursing the infant of a campmate who had died—*I still have milk, and the baby is so small*—but she never again mentioned Latvia or the farm.

III

ONCE THERE was a time when the living made a habit of sitting with the newly dead. The dead would be offered a special chair, and everyone would crowd around to ask the dead: Why did you leave this world? Then, all the living would call out in turn the reasons they believed the dead should remain with them. When they ran out of things to say, or they could no longer keep their eyes open for want of sleep, the living would place the body of the dead in its coffin. Next, they set plates of food on the table, especially beans and peas, said to mimic the shape of tears. And then, before they turned out the lights and went to bed, the living would lift the coffin's lid and leave it partway off, so that the dead could get up in the night if it desired, and have one last meal alone. In the morning, the living joined the dead for breakfast, plates on knees, or balanced on the coffin's edge. The grandmothers saved their best bites to place on the plate of the dead. Your road is long, so long, they would say. Here is some strength for what's ahead. And whatever beer or bread was left, they took to the barn, to sprinkle in the cows' stalls, so the herd could mourn, too.

The old ways held that the dead never stopped being considered members of the family, and it was up to the living to try and impress upon the dead this fact.

For the first few years after she died, I waited for my grand-mother, Livija, to visit me, as her mother had done for her, but she never came. I said her name to myself at night, when I couldn't sleep, like a summons—thinking of how, if I said it as an English speaker would, the first syllable sounded like "live," as in the command form of the verb "to live," the "j" soft, voiced like the letter "y": *LIV-ee-yah*. And if I pronounced it the Latvian way, the first syllable sounded like the word "leave," as in "to leave someone."

I had asked for a few of her things in the hope they might serve as talismans to my grief: a calla lily spaded from her gar-den's soil; her old mixing bowl, in which she soaked threads of saffron in warm milk to color the sweet dough she braided to celebrate our birthdays and name days; a velvet evening gown from the 1970s, soft as sable, the color of crushed violets, cop-ied from an image in *Vogue*. It didn't fit me and I didn't want it to; my grandmother, a talented seamstress who could sew without patterns, and whose stitches were so precise that her garments could be worn inside out, had tailored the gown so perfectly to her own form, that even hanging in my closet, it returned to the world the shape and weight of the space that I had known her physical body to occupy.

And while these things gave her absence a kind of presence in my life, they could not help me picture her with the kind of clarity that would make her feel real to me again, complicated and full, more than these fading traces of memory: the brown of her eyes, irises edged in blue, like the bark of a madrone tree set against a clear sky; the way she smelled of sunlight, clothing left to dry on the line; the shape of her curlers beneath the kerchiefs she wore home each week after having her hair set at Sharon's Beauty Parlor—a double-wide trailer located in the motor court tucked behind the neighborhood corner store that did brisk trade in both penny candy and adult magazines; the angry divots her clip-on earrings left when unclasped; the sound of her body, released from its girdle, soft and low, like the exhalation of air that releases a dandelion of its seeds; the method she employed to test a bolt of fabric before committing to buy it: grabbing a handful of material and clenching it in her fist for several seconds. No good, she would say. Wrinkles too easily. It will look old and worn before you leave the house!

She tried to learn to drive—once. She crushed the neighbor's fence beneath the back wheels of the car. After that, if my grandfather was not home, she walked anywhere she needed to go.

She could peel an apple without ever lifting her knife, the fruit unwound from itself in gentle drifts in the bottom of her kitchen sink.

Come here, she would say, when I woke and complained of cold, opening her bathrobe as if it was her skin, and letting me slip inside.

Sometimes, when we went shopping together, clerks would insist they did not understand what she was trying to say, even as they bit back laughter, and she tried so hard to stay calm, composed, in her handmade clothes. Unwrinkled.

I hate them for this still.

The problem was that my memories of her were now reduced to little more than anecdotes, lists, not the true sense of a life, complicated, evolving, embedded in an unfolding present.

At the same time, it had also grown harder for me to locate my grandmother in our shared version of her past.

I tried to find her again in the stories that she had left to me of the farm, but they felt brittle now, unfamiliar, all the things that had gone unspoken, the absences and elisions and silences so much more apparent now that I was forced to encounter them on my own.

It didn't help to recruit my father. Although he had grown up hearing many of the same stories, and he had come to the United States when he was still young enough that he could switch between English and Latvian without accent, to call back what he knew of the family's history, his memories of growing up in the refugee camps, in any language, caused him real pain. So he held back the words.

He told me once that he remembered a stretch in his adolescence when he could not speak without stuttering. His brother and his younger sister recalled their own periods of stammering, too.

It wasn't that my father and his siblings didn't want to hear their mother's stories, or weren't interested in them. For a long time, they simply did not know. Recently, my father's younger sister, who had been just a year old when the family arrived in the United States, told me she did not learn of the details of her mother's flight from Latvia until after she had graduated from high school, until after she had left the house, and even then, the details were scant.

In my father's case, it seemed to me that his reluctance to engage with the family history felt almost protective, as if to place himself inside of it again—to investigate the deliberate silences that it contained, the home that had been left behind, the hole where his father's eye should have been, the missing months of his own infancy, set against the war's end—might actually hold a personal danger. I use the word *danger* because on the rare occasions he attempted to enter these spaces, to look directly into them, he was quickly overcome, and would shut down, as if the past traumas he had been exposed to were not something that he had survived, but something still happening, the present-tense intensity of it all too much to bear.

When my grandparents returned to Latvia for their first and only visit after the war, after Latvia regained its independence, my father had gone with them.

To this day, he cannot speak of the experience without crying, finally seeing the country he had left before he could ever know it, visiting the region where his mother and father were raised, living according to its rhythms, staying long enough to begin to work alongside his relatives, helping to lay a new roof on the barn, collecting honey from the hives. And yet, once the trip was over and my father was back home, it was almost as if the emotional force of what he had experienced frightened him in some way, and he retreated deep inside himself.

He didn't consider returning to Latvia again for twenty years, not until I began to travel there, and although I know he felt a deep and abiding love for the relatives he had met and lived alongside, he had not been able to bring himself to write or to call them in all that time.

I don't know why I find it so hard, he told me once. Why I can't break out of my shell, sometimes. What is the Latvian word for hermit?

Years later, I would recognize my father in a story a colleague once told me about visiting a facility where those who had seen war were treated for severe post-traumatic stress. Of all the things she saw and heard, the woman said, what haunted her still was the way staff approached anyone who appeared in genuine anguish. Always, they started with the same question, gentle but insistent: *Where are you right now?*

Not to remind the patients of where their bodies were, but to acknowledge that our memories are real places in which it is possible to become trapped.

The woman and I worked together at the same newspaper as reporters.

It was the only job I had ever spoken of wanting since I was in grade school, already so comfortable inhabiting a history that was not my own, that even then, when asked what I wanted to do when I grew up, I claimed a living that would allow me to observe the living of others.

I slipped business cards behind screen doors, the name of the paper I worked for on one side, a scribbled note on the other: *I am truly sorry about ——. If you ever feel like talking about the life that was lost, I'm here to listen.* I said this regularly to strangers, never once considering whether this was something that I should instead be saying to myself.

It's interesting to me now to think that I had deliberately chosen a profession where I was actively discouraged from ever using the word *I*, from ever inserting myself in the frame.

And yet, in the years following my grandmother's death, I found myself writing different versions of the same story over and over again.

Of abandoned amusement parks, where elk now grazed in what had once been the parking lot, where sedge and Scotch broom slowly swallowed all evidence of the log flume ride, the snack shack, the miniature train.

Of a house where a room on the second floor had been converted into an aviary by a man who had discovered the thrumming of birds' wings was the only thing that could distract him from his despair. Until one day, it couldn't anymore. And still, as his ex-wife sorted through his remaining things, the sparrows winged in circles around the room, empty, except for a single chair, positioned so you could imagine him sitting, alone, taking in the arc of their flight, night after night.

Of a bench in the city's oldest park, dedicated to a man who once climbed to its highest point, and as the sun began to drop in the sky, drenched himself in lighter fluid, then flinted a match. *Come sit*, says a sign on the bench, *And know that you are loved.* A sign that also bears the inscription of the man's name, and an engraving of a dove, because, and this is not written there, but can be learned only by tracing the sign back to his mother, who put it there, for someone, anyone, to find, and to ask, so she could remember once more:

> [He] was my firstborn, and you know, I was so tired, I would cradle him and talk to him and I thought I was calling him love, but after a while, I realized, I'm so tired I'm saying dove. But then I thought, what's so wrong with that. Dove is beautiful too. So I called him my dove.

I wrote these stories as if secretly assembling a list of locations where it was difficult to distinguish the boundaries between what had been taken away from this world and what remained.

I wrote:

> We are surrounded by invisible cities, places constructed entirely of memory, of suggestion: the remnants of a foundation, broken slabs of concrete, a clearing in a field, an unusually ordered stand of trees.

I wrote, in other words, like a person trying to assure herself that the shape of what was missing could be used to rebuild that which she didn't even know she'd lost.

AND THEN, at last, my grandmother came to me, just not in the way I had expected.

One night, my father brought over a box of items that he'd found while cleaning the last of the things from my grandparents' house, where he had gone to live following the end of his second marriage.

These were things which did not seem to have any discernible value, but which he could not bring himself to give away. He wondered if I might have any use for them.

Inside, I found spools of silken thread; a music box with a pull-string that my grandmother had played to calm me when she lay me down for afternoon naps on her bed; and a yellow and green scarf, clearly woven by hand.

My father said he had found the scarf deep in one of my grandmother's dresser drawers. It was old, fraying in places. I had never seen her wear it in all the years I knew her. But it still smelled of her and so I took it.

Later, while going through some old photographs, I found one that had been taken in my grandparents' Riga apartment not long before she fled Latvia. I had always understood that almost nothing from my grandparents' old life had survived, that my grandmother had emerged from her journey along the war roads with only the clothes she happened to be wearing the day she fled.

But as soon as I saw the photograph, I recognized it: the scarf.

It was unmistakable, knotted at the hollow of my grandmother's throat.

Where once stories had seemed the only way to access her past, now, suddenly, something tangible had surfaced, pointing the way back to where it all began: proof of what could be made and unmade, then made again; the complexity of the pattern invisible only until you sit still long enough to follow the unraveling threads, retrace their individual paths, so many intricate connections, gifted to you by the silent, insistent hands of the dead.

IV

THE WOMAN who could be my grandmother, but is not, motions for me to follow her into the weary house.

I can hear the chirruping of a bad hip as she hitches slowly down the narrow hallway, which is lined with tomato starts and baskets of flower bulbs, white with bonemeal, knobbly with dirt and age. As she leads me into what appears to be a sitting room, I see her draw a balled-up handkerchief from the cuff of her cardigan and dab it at her eyes—eyes that I must keep convincing myself are not, in fact, my grandmother's eyes. My grandmother Livija's eyes were brown, edged in blue, I remind myself. This woman's are blue, edged in brown.

She scrapes a chair back from the table, indicates I should sit.

It's easier for her to let photographs speak.

Here, she says, wresting a thick album from a cabinet in the corner of the room. She sets it on the table between us, lifts away the yellowing layers of parchment that cover each face like a caul.

Livija, she says. And my grandmother appears to us, a young woman, the hem of her skirt hovering above the summer-stiffened grass, her face turned slightly as if she registered the sound of her name.

Next to her, a boy buttoned into a suit as rigid and unyielding as the fence posts in front of which they pose, itching neck and rakish grin stifled—*Janis!*—said just like that, an exclamation, the sound of uncontained braying, my grandmother's brother.

So this must be you? I ask, pointing to a little girl who sits on a chair between the other two in the photograph. Her hair is pulled into braids, her feet end in stiff boots. She looks like she has been swinging them back and forth. She nods.

Ausma. It means dawn or daybreak in Latvian. A lightening. My grandmother's sister, born when my grandmother, Livija, was fourteen, and whom I have specifically traveled here to meet, my *history in flesh and blood.*

Was this portrait taken at the farm? I ask Ausma.

Yes, she says.

My grandmother told me all about the farm, I say.

Ausma doesn't immediately respond.

It sounded like an incredible place, I say.

She flips a page. I can hear a clock somewhere in the house, its second hand conducting the tiny eternity that has opened up between us.

You should know that your grandmother's stories aren't my stories, Ausma says at last. Her memories aren't my memories.

For years, people had asked me when I finally planned to visit the Latvia of my grandmother's stories, and I always had an excuse ready, about work, about money.

It didn't occur to me then that my hesitancy might have had more to do with fear—specifically, the fear that such a trip, rather than confirming the general outlines of the memories my grandmother had gifted me, could only, inevitably, complicate them.

FRIENDS OFTEN WANT to know what that first visit was like, what it felt like in that instant to be reunited with long lost family. And I always wonder whether my answer is too quiet to make sense to anyone else—we sat, I say, we sat, and we wept, and we ate, and we laughed, and we ate, and we wept some more—but it is the instant recognition I felt in the presence of that quiet, something continuous, vital, enduring, the assumed natural state of things, that I always return to; a memory of such pure and overwhelming contentment, a sense of peace, unlike anything I had ever known in my life before, that I wonder if I do understand something of the intensity of the memories that have kept my father from speaking, the intensity of a past that feels as if it is still happening inside of us.

Go ahead. Ask me:

Where are you right now?

Here is what I would tell you:

I'm sitting. I'm sitting at a table. I'm sitting at a table with Ausma and her husband, a man named Harijs, who, although he is in his mideighties, has just been scrambling around on the roof, checking for a possible leak.

Do you know how many times I should have died? he asks, as he takes my hands in his hands, tar-stained, stretched by years of labor to the size of bear traps, triggered, lying flat.

Shh, says Ausma, poking him, though not unkindly. Not now.

We are joined by two of Ausma and Harijs's three children, and their children's children. Also at the table that day is the family's first great-grandchild, a girl, just turned two, and when I hear her name for the first time, I have to ask the family to repeat it because it sounds so much like my grandmother's name: Liva. We are seated like this, so many generations, so close to one another, that every voice seems to begin inside my own chest. My lips are swollen from shots of sweet muscat, or maybe it is the salt of my own tears. Eat, someone says. Drink, someone else says. Hours pass. There is no room to walk around the table where we toast and cry and eat and laugh, so Liva crawls across my lap to reach her grandmother— Ausma's youngest daughter, my second cousin, a woman named Ligita, who upon seeing me for the first time, ran forward and embraced me so fiercely that I felt my own ribs under the pressure of her forearms, work-strong, sunned to the color of cloves. We've waited for you, she said, as she held me. We waited, and now you're really here.

I can feel Ausma studying me from her place across the table, and whenever I meet her gaze, I read her expression as one of overwhelming happiness, but also great sorrow, as if in me she recognizes someone temporarily restored to her, but also still lost. I, in turn, study Ausma. Her hair, downy as a catkin, combed so quickly I can still trace the pass of each tine. Her skin is remarkably smooth, like tumbled stone. Only her forehead is rifted and seamed—the kind of furrowing that is the result of sustained intensity, stress, exhaustion. She downs a single glass of sweet wine, presses a knuckle to her lips to stifle a belch, then winks at me. In some ways, she feels lighter than I ever remember my grandmother being, less restrained somehow. Like someone who keeps her sweetness and joy close to the surface, but also her anger, I think, looking at her hands, nicked and seamed with the white of old wounds, never stitched, left instead to find their own way to close. The kind of anger that helps a person stay alive.

Tea? someone asks.

And as we wait for the scream of the kettle, Ausma decides now is the perfect time to take me to meet the rest of our dead.

Out comes her album again, and she flips through the pages with the solemn efficiency of a tour guide tasked with escorting me through my unknown past: a wave to the ancient fraternity of grandfathers, leather-skinned and possessed of an uncanny knowledge of the cultivation of facial hair; the godmothers of names long forgotten; men dressed in uniforms for wars that were fought for sides she cannot recall.

Once, briefly, my great-great-grandmother steps out to meet us, ghostly, so faint even Ausma is momentarily unconvinced of her existence—*I think that's my grandmother, yes, no, yes*. . . . A skirted figure, sitting in the gloom of what appears to be an agricultural shed; clearer is the lamb she holds by its two front legs, tender belly exposed to us, the legs blurred, kicking. Its appearance is followed by a succession of wedding dresses, white as the lamb's pelt, empire-waisted, drop-waisted, each, regardless of the era, modeled by an unsmiling woman who also wears the Latvian bride's traditional crown of flowers.

Did my grandmother have a wedding photograph? I ask.

Ausma does not seem to hear me.

Here is my wedding photograph! she says. I was sad because my dress got dirty and my roses were wilting.

Now she is taking me to see the corpses.

Formal funeral portraits: the body in its casket, the casket borne on the shoulders of the grieving to the cemetery plot. But first, this is where the body was laid out, in the front yard, under the linden trees, amid heaps of cut flowers. Covered in a white linen sheet, only the face is exposed, already hollowing in death, collapsing along its ridges, sinking like a roof staved by snow. Suited and kerchiefed, the grieving circle the body at the photographer's instructions. And then—his flash. In this instant, all eyes are turned to the body. The body's face already turned toward home.

And then, a new page.

Where is this? I ask, pointing to a portrait of Ausma, her mother, and brother. They are posing with another couple in a room with rough white walls, the dull brass of what appears to be a bed frame visible in the background, a single potted plant, hunched over, embarrassed, trying to shed its dropsied leaves. The women in the photograph all look off to the left, as if avoiding eye contact with the photographer. The men look directly into the lens.

And the Ausma who is here with me in this little dining room with a view to the surrounding pastures, empty now of cows, is making her way back there, too—I can feel it—as if she has pushed away from the table and shuffled out the front door, past the flea-gnawing dogs, the cats dug into the cool dirt beneath the cherry trees, across fields and through forests, heading deep into the wilds of her memories, emerging, finally, when she has reached the girl in that photograph.

She regards herself.

I'm in Siberia, she says.

Later, in the state archives in Riga, I will find hundreds

of photographs like the one Ausma showed me of the white-walled room in Siberia, the same composition, but different faces, the work of enterprising itinerant photographers who roamed the region's remote settlements, proposing to snap the portraits of the exiles who lived there in exchange for whatever they could offer in return. Scavenged berries. Socks. Sewing needles fashioned from fish bones. For the exiles, it was worth the sacrifice of their most precious commodities. Portraits offered proof of life. They resurrected the banished, restored them to sight, so that it was possible to imagine they existed once more in the world of the living. In some of the portraits, I notice the women are wearing a similar dress. It takes me a while to realize that it probably is the same dress, passed from one exile to another so that each might feel she looks her best for the photographer.

Who is the couple? I ask Ausma.

They were our neighbors there, Ausma says. Latvians, too. They came on the same train.

I study their faces. The woman wears a kerchief, which, according to the old ways, means she is married, but she looks more like the mother or even the grandmother of the man who stands protectively behind the chair where she sits. Her breasts are heavy, finishing in her lap. She grips one hand with the other, her fingers tensed, clawed. Her chin juts forward in the way of someone who has lost all her teeth, her mouth soft, quaggy, like a field after weeks of rain.

She had a baby, Ausma says. A newborn, just a few weeks old. It died on the way.

Ausma pushes up from the table, leaving me with the album, and shuffles off.

Then quietly, over her shoulder, as if an afterthought:

One of the guards took the body from her, then threw it out the doors of the train.

To be part of a family is to know instinctively the subtleties behind what remains unsaid and why.

And yet, with my new, long lost family, it was clear that I still had so much more to learn.

About Ausma and Siberia, and what happened to her after my grandmother left Latvia.

But also, the farm.

I had assumed someone from our family must still be living at Lembi, because I had not heard otherwise. And yet, since my arrival, no one had brought it up, or suggested that we go there, and I could sense the silence surrounding it is something soft, vulnerable, like the things that are revealed when an old log is lifted.

I didn't know enough yet to intuit the outlines of what was not there—though I had begun to suspect Siberia and the farm were somehow psychically linked, in a way that makes one silence impossible to understand outside the context of the other.

And so, I decided, at last, to ask if someone could take me to Lembi.

In the quiet that follows, I can hear the shrilling of sparrows outside, the exaggerated yipping of a puppy. Through the window, I glimpse the dog's silhouette: pawing and biting at the shadows the birds cast as they swoop over the lawn. The puppy belongs to Ligita and her husband, Aivars, a man with the ability to cultivate the kind of mustache the ancient fathers from the photographs would have admired, and an encyclopedic knowledge of what it means to be self-sufficient, down to milling his own wood by hand in a shed at the back of his house. The puppy is a German shepherd who was found abandoned, starving, in the parking lot of a nearby hamlet where Ligita works as a bookkeeper, signing checks for pensioners, writing receipts for library fines paid in change.

Gone, I think I hear someone say over the cries of the dog and the birds.

I wait for more. But the silence continues to extend between us, drifting like a fine mist of wood released by Aivars's saw, until it occurs to me that no one feels comfortable giving me the words for what this means, that they need me to discover it on my own.

I'm just curious about the place where my grandmother grew up, I say. I have no other expectations, if you could just show me the way. And at that, the room seems to contract with relief.

Off to the car we trundle, including the baby, tiny Liva, shod in rubber boots, trying with unbending knees to outtrot the puppy who pursues her, openmouthed, grinning, desperate to lash her with its tongue. As we back down the driveway, he dances in place, dribbling pee, trying to contain the torture he feels at being left behind.

From the car window we see storks, gliding to standing in the overwintered fields, legs the color of the hottest coals puncturing the last riming seal of snow. Here: smoke hanging above a chimney, weak, bowing, like the vertebrae of a grandmother with bad back. There: a pile of hay, gray with rot. A cat, belly-crawling through the mud, stopping to shake its paws with the fervor of someone trying to revive feeling in cold-numbed extremities. A woman, balanced on stacked heels, cell phone in hand, taking the brunt of the debris kicked up by the wheels of the car on her bare legs, headed down a stretch of road where there are only fields. An old man, glimpsed briefly, deep in a forested stretch—untamed woods, pathless—tugging a grocery cart.

When the car finally stops, we step out into a landscape that holds only still air, the hush of a place that has begun to forget what it is to hold a conversation with anyone other than itself.

And then, the house emerges from behind a screen of weeds.

I recognize it, in the way that one can sometimes briefly recognize, in the faces of the very elderly, all the versions of every age they have ever been.

From the outside, it is exactly as my grandmother described—there is the window in front of which she and her brother and sister posed for their portraits.

And now the stories are returning to me: there is the stoop from which my grandmother's mother would have shouted for her to stop playing in the hemp fields, where my grandmother sometimes liked to sneak on hot days, the smell of the sun on the leaves like something sweet and something dead, all at once.

And there is the half of the house where Livija's father's elderly cousin would have lived with his wife, a woman said to have lacked the will to contain her chickens, who let them run everywhere, pecking and scratching like a mad herd, sharing their mites, laying, without qualm, in their cousin-chickens' nests, until no one could say whose eggs were whose or whose chicks were whose.

And so then it would have been behind this wall, on the opposite half of the house, when, one day, in frustration, my grandmother's mother would issue an ultimatum, the repercussions of which would drift far into the future, like a feather from one of the marauding poultry next door snatched up by the wind: *Do whatever you have to. Buy up their share of the land. Promise to care for them to the end of their days. But those people and their chickens have to go.* And because sixteen and a half hectares of dirt seemed, at the time, a small price to see something other than her back in the night, her husband agreed.

I study the front door, which still hangs easy in its jamb. It feels as if it could have just been slammed shut—maybe on an angry tom, tail switching, stolen milk still wetting his chin, or maybe on a man off to negotiate the exile of his cousin and his chickens from the land.

And I'm thinking how remarkable it is that the house still appears to hold the shape of its memories, when I begin to register that something is, in fact, off, like a person who tells a passable story, only to repeat the same story a few minutes later, unaware of what he has forgotten, of what is skipping inside him.

I skirt the edge of the house, and as I approach its flank, that's when I see what has previously remained hidden: something has gored the roof. Slivers of wood, greasy strands of insulation dangle at the edges of the hole like flaps of cartilage.

Back here, it smells of larvaed water, steaming animal.

All the while, the family leaves me alone to my discovery.

They stand at a respectful distance, at the edge of the property, where the last of the unmelted snow has drifted into swells, rock-studded and stubborn, resistant to the thin sun.

I'm grateful that they didn't try to define the scope of the loss for me.

And I can feel myself crying before I can register why.

At first, I think it's because I'm mourning the fact that I've come too late, that I will never step into a real-life version of my grandmother's re-created idyll.

But then it occurs to me that I am, in fact, crying in the way someone does when she is relieved of a burden.

What had Ausma said?

Your grandmother's stories aren't my stories.

And when she'd first said it, it had made me sad, frightened even, that there would be no way for me to make the pieces of the past fit together in any kind of way that would return it to something whole.

EACH SUMMER when I was a child, my grandparents sent me to the forest to search for a way back to our lost country. For two weeks, every year, until I was in my midteens, I attended a camp designed to immerse the children and grandchildren of the local Latvian refugees in a living version of the refugees' collective memories of home.

Conjured from the woods of Washington State, the camp sat on property purchased with pooled funds—a real estate transaction within the local refugee community's reach because the land, while beautiful, abutted a state correctional institute.

There, in cool stands of evergreen, I dressed in folk costumes and learned traditional folk dances and wove bookmarks

by hand in the colors of the Latvian flag, which we raised each
morning while solemnly singing the national anthem. English
was prohibited. I remember doing a spirited session of aero-
bics one afternoon—all the instructions yipped in Latvian. On
this subject, camp rules were strict: each English word uttered
meant ten push-ups on the spot, and we all lived in fear of
being called out in this way, of ending up facedown in the dirt.

Occasionally, exceptions were made, such as for the music
to which we learned to dance, my hands on a boy's bony cow-
hips, our teachers shouting *one, two, three, one, two, three*, in
Latvian, as we twitched a dizzy polka to Abba's *Greatest Hits*.

At the end of each day, after the sun had set, we circled the
dying campfire, clad in our Nikes and OP shorts and stink-
ing of bug spray, and we clasped hands and swayed and sang
a sad, slow folk song begging the wind to carry us back to the
shores of Latvia. Then we crawled into our beds in dormi-
tories built to look like replicas of the old wooden houses of
the countryside, like Lembi, that the refugees had abandoned
when they fled.

The camp's lake held crawfish in its shallows, their shed
skins skimming the shore, cracking beneath our curled toes;
but also, leeches, which we learned to unlatch from our bodies
with the touch of lit matches.

Inara loves summer camp, my grandmother wrote to the relatives in Latvia, *but she says her least favorite thing is swimming*.

On land, there were lessons in how to identify old farm imple-
ments, oral histories of the proper mounding of hay, instruction
in the selection of wildflowers appropriate to the braided crowns
worn by maidens on midsummer's night.

Our counselors crafted elaborate living reenactments of

fairy tales and pagan myths, sending us on rambling quests through the forest, where we would encounter costumed devils and witches who we would then be forced to outwit in feats of cunning and skill, or to dispatch with the properly recited tone poem.

In this way, year after year, we came to believe the past was a place that would always wait for us.

We were too young to know that there is a difference between the exile's memory of home, which remains perfectly still, immobile, as if encased in a carapace, and a homeland's memory of itself, which drags itself from the shallows each day, molted, tender, new.

AND NOW the sun is sagging, snagging on the tips of the pines, making what is left of Lembi appear as if illuminated from within, the fading light finding every breach.

There's an awful beauty to this moment, arriving, finally, at the scene of one's past, and discovering only ruin. And yet, ruin resists simple affirmation, forces us to place questions over certainties, to surrender what we had imagined had always existed, to ask instead, what if.

What if: the most accurate resurrection of our histories depends not on their preservation, but on their constant, quiet disassembly.

What if: we told ourselves that ruin is really a reclaiming, a natural revision of what's always been assumed.

What if: I had come here sooner. There would have been more for me to see. But maybe less for me to find.

From somewhere behind me, I hear the baby stomp and squeal.

When I turn to look, she is reaching for something balanced in the crook of a sapling: a nest, abandoned, fraying.

In ruin, edges vanish. Everything touches.

She is, it occurs to me, the same age I was when I went to live with my grandmother.

V

How do you feel? my husband asks me, after that first visit.

Like my DNA is singing, I say.

Do you think a country can be a mother? a friend writes, when she hears I've already booked a return ticket to Latvia, to Gulbene, to what is left of the farm that makes me feel like I can see for once both what has been taken, but also what has been left. Can land mother? Can it replace a mother?

I knew you'd come back, says Ausma, when she sees me again, for the second time in just a year, but she is crying with such force that it occurs to me she didn't know that I'd come back. And I think that I might have just learned one of the saddest things I will ever know: that nearly a century of experience can teach you to believe more fervently in the certainty of what will disappear than the possibility of what can be restored.

———

But then, that is the way of things when you make your home in a place where loss is inscribed on the landscape, from the trunks of its trees, to the waters in its lakes.

Like the pine that grows in a pasture at the crossroads that once marked the way to Gulbene's old cemetery, just a short walk from Ausma's house.

There was a time when people came to this pine on their way to bury their dead. I will come to learn that Ausma, in fact, stopped here on the day they carried her father's casket to the town cemetery. Tongues numb with vodka, the mourners stood at the pine's trunk and drew knives down its bark, a cross for each soul. It's said that they imagined that the hole that they made would bind their loss to something in this world that endured, and would give their grief a home.

Maybe this is why, all these years later, local people still know the location of the pine, even if no one goes there anymore on burial days, and most people have long ago forgotten that anyone did. Why they erect a shin-high fence at its base in anticipation of the visitors who will somehow find their way to this pasture, despite a lack of signs or clear directions.

Up close, the pine is not a particularly compelling specimen on its own. It holds its spindly branches at awkward angles and does not possess great height. But it is remarkable not for what it possesses, but because of what is gone, the way the living bark still bears the shape of each loss; hundreds of tiny hatch marks.

Then there's the lake where locals go to stand on the shore and stare at the water's wrinkled surface so that they might catch a glimpse of nothing.

The lake's bottom is said to be the site of a phantom village that no one can ever see. An entire town swallowed up one day, when the lake suddenly arrived, unannounced, to find people already living in what it believed was its appointed place. And no one saw the lake's waters rushing in to claim what the lake insisted was rightfully its home—the town's inhabitants too busy celebrating the wedding of two locals, they didn't have time, mid-toast, mid-dance, skirts raised, to register their own drowning.

And this is one small tale. But it is also a version of the larger truth. This has always been such an easy place to disappear.

One day, the neighbors are out in their fields, hitching the draft horse to the plow, or bringing straw to the sow soon to farrow. The next day, there is no sign of them, the farmhouse door thrown open, the cows screaming to be milked. Maybe it's something to do with the transport trucks carrying people to rail depots. Or maybe it is the mounds that appear suddenly deep in the forest, black earth hastily tamped down over moss. And those who remain—they never say a word, as if they believe to say something is to invite their own deletion, quick as the point of a knife scratching away pine bark. Better to stay quiet, pretend you are focused on such things as bedding down the barn stalls, the hushing and rustling of the straw as it falls from your hands producing a sound that you could easily mistake for *stillhere*.

Spend any amount of time in Latvia, and you will quickly discover that every family's history is cratered with epochs of loss and displacement, sudden chasms of nothing.

Consider the last century—a random almanac of vanishing:

1905

People deported to Siberia following an attempted revolution: **3,000**

1915–1917

Latvian conscripts killed fighting for the Russian army in World War I: **32,000**

1917

Number of Latvian refugees driven to neighboring countries by the fighting of World War I: **1,000,000**

June 1941

Men, women and children deported to Siberia over the course of two days by Soviet order: **15,000**

July–October 1942

Jewish Latvians murdered by German troops—and fellow Latvians: **70,000**

1941–1944

Jews brought to Latvia during World War II from other European countries to be killed: **20,000**

1944

Estimated number of Latvians who fled the country at the end of World War II for the West: **250,000**

1945

Estimated number of civilians killed, unaccounted for by war's end: **200,000**

March 1949
Latvians deported to Siberia over the span of
three days by Soviet order: 41,000

Today, the disappearing continues, although this time it comes in the form of a one-way ticket booked for England—but really, the final destination could just as easily be Ireland or Germany or Spain or Norway, flight paths traced each year by thousands of men and women who board planes in search of work, and never come back.

The country's population is declining, like a clock running backwards.

Over the past ten years, 250,000 people have been erased from all official tallies. For years, Latvia's citizens have vanished at a rate of 68 people a day. There are no signs of reversal, and on some days, even the government cannot summon the resolve to craft optimistic denials. *Latvia*, pronounced a minister for the Office of Family and Children, *is dying out.*

In the countryside, where life is set to the schedule of milking and the local papers are attuned to the slightest fluctuations in the welfare of the potato crops ("Beetles Attack!" read the front page of the local paper one week), the dying looks like this:

In June, on solstice, when tradition calls for a bonfire to burn through the night, those still left in the countryside search the horizon for purls of smoke.

The old people remember a time when it seemed hundreds of fires blazed in the dark. Now, they struggle to spot the faintest smudge of one pyre in the distance, maybe two.

Used to be they sent people to Siberia, a local dairy farmer will tell me. Now they just exile themselves.

———

THE PUPPY RECOGNIZES ME as soon as he sees me again, the pads of his paws skritching my collarbone when he jumps and tries to force me into a happy jig. Liva, the baby who found the nest, is no longer a baby, but the sister to a baby. The big-puppy licks food from the new great-grandchild's face.

I have come back so that I can be here for the span of a summer, the time of light, hours and hours of an unsetting sun that tricks the heart into thinking that it will never tire or slow.

What do you want to do while you are here, Ligita, Ausma's youngest daughter, asks as she embraces me again with the kind of enveloping fierceness that is meant to banish all distance in an instant.

And I tell her this is the closest I imagine I can ever come to experiencing life as my grandmother might have known it, and so all I want to do with the time that I have here, in Gulbene, with them, is to live, as family lives together.

So we live.

We live outside, harvesting tomatoes, snicking weeds from the potato beds, wrenching beetles from the leaves.

There are trips deep into the forest to forage for wild fruit and mushrooms. We emerge with baskets of chanterelles and Latvian huckleberries, our limbs burred with bug bites, dense swarms of mosquitoes that reach us through our clothing, clog each breath.

I see, for the first time, with Aivars's help, the dimpled tracks of wild boar.

I harvest strawberries and currants from the garden until the palms of my hands are leathered and red, as if burned by lye.

At night, in the undark, I follow the smoke to a former cowshed that has been converted into a sauna.

I take water from a bucket in which birch branches soak and let the drops pearl onto the hot rocks.

Then, I hit myself with the moistened birch switches until the leaves drift the floor and my skin shines like peeled bark.

This is how we mark time:

First, we cut armfuls of peonies. Then dahlias. Then gladiolus.

And with each new day, a little more of what had seemed lost finds its way back to me.

TODAY WE ARE TALKING about love. And a boy. No, not a boy—a baby rabbit, Ausma says. A baby rabbit hiding in the back row of desks that thicketed her childhood schoolhouse. So little, Ausma remembers. Quiet. Always listening. Ears twitching.

That was her first impression of her husband, Harijs.

Was there a romance back then? I ask.

Not for me, no, but he seemed to think so, she says, and smiles. I didn't even know his name.

This has become our routine, to talk in the mornings about the time before now as Ausma clears the breakfast dishes. Ausma offering strands of stories that I gather, one at a time, and I try to find a way to make them hold together in my mind, like my grandmother's scarf, which is up in my room, under my pillow.

I thought no one would marry me; I was in Siberia during the years all my friends married, Ausma says.

I don't stop her to ask more about Siberia, although I want to. Something tells me to go slowly.

And then, says Ausma, after we were allowed to come back, and I was working at the chicken farm, he came over to help my brother, and he saw me sawing something. He said he was so impressed by how hard I worked. Well, I had some experience cutting wood back in Siberia, I said. I know, he said. And I said, how did you know that? And he said because we went to school together. I said, we went to school together? How did you remember me? Later, he told me he'd always thought of me, that he was quiet when we were younger because he was paying attention, memorizing things about me, but he was too young then to dare to do what he wanted to do now. And that was to tell me that he didn't want to let me slip away again.

So he waited for you all those years? I ask.

He waited, she says, and smiles, then pinches Harijs's arm just beneath his T-shirt.

I waited, he says.

They held their wedding party here, at the house they still live in, in the garden. We can see the spot from the kitchen window.

Do you know, I built this house, Harijs tells me. With my own hands! And then I wished for the perfect bride to always keep me company in this house, and she appeared!

They filled the fields with music from a record player they planted in the grass beneath a canopy of lilac trees, and everyone danced, while my great-grandmother sat bundled on a bench, happily summoning mittens from skeins of wool, soft as a baby rabbit's pelt.

I knew there were people whispering, that I was old to marry, that we would be lucky to have children, Ausma says. *Ha!* And I had three. Now we have grandchildren, even great-grandchildren.

She is my love, Harijs says.

And I am struck by not just the sweet simple clarity of his declaration, but also its construction:

Here in this little house that Harijs built by hand for his love, she is, he is, we are.

It is a sweet simple life, focused on the present. The next meal is what we can gather from the garden. There is no indoor shower, only a sauna. And a privy.

Always, with breakfast, lunch or dinner, there is dessert: stewed fruit, whipped semolina with fresh cream or maybe the extravagance of candy plucked from the village supermarket's penny bins.

And always, in the afternoon, *quiet hour*.

Rest, Inara, rest, Ausma will insist. Don't read. Don't talk. Just rest.

Then, when we rise, more work until we can't work anymore: raking, mowing, baking, butchering the hank of wild boar that Aivars has dropped by.

The weather is central to our day. We talk about it endlessly.

It looks like it will rain this afternoon, Ausma says, eyeing the sky, her cleaver momentarily suspended over a bloody swine hock. We'd better pick the last of the peas.

One day, during quiet hour, I take Ausma's photo album to the room with me. And I notice that in pages toward the back, the old photographs begin to give way to more recent ones, including photographs of our family my grandmother must have sent from the States after the sisters were once again able to reestablish contact.

Ausma has laid out her sister's photographs so that they are engaged in a kind of conversation with her own: here are pictures of Ausma's children on one side of the page, Livija's on the other; their Christmas, our Christmas; Ausma posing in front of a horse, my grandmother posing in front of my grandfather's Chrysler K car; here is Ausma, helping to carry a casket, covered in pine boughs, here is my grandmother casting a handful of dirt on my grandfather's grave.

And then I notice that one of the photos has come loose and fluttered to the floor. When I go to retrieve it, I can see my grandmother has penciled a brief description on the back.

Emils took this picture just as Juris was sneezing.

I check all the other photos of our family, and each one is the same: a brief vignette of nothing.

Here we are at Crater Lake. Maruta so wanted to go home, but we were 400 miles away.

My dahlias. It has been raining and I have had a hard time keeping up with the weeds. Look how scraggly.

Baby Inara with my little dog Polly. Polly attacked the vacuum cleaner because it got too close to Inara!

For a long time afterward, I think of my grandmother's captions, how hard she tried with each one to convey the kind of intimacy that distance steals from the separated, the seemingly unremarkable moments of everyday lives.

It is what I think about when Ausma and I are debating which sweet we should have with our lunch: stewed gooseberries with whipped cream? (Maybe that's better with breakfast, Ausma decides.)

It is what I think about when we roam the house, hunting flies (Ausma keeping count: 21! Swatter whizzing. 22!). When we practice English (*Dead. Fly.*). When we watch the nightly national news and both swear we are not tired, and then fall asleep sitting up during the segments on vandalized red light cameras outside Riga or preparations for the next national song festival, Ausma with her latest favorite kitten from the barn curled up high on her chest, like a fur stole. Or when, together, we clean the family cemetery plot, dragging rags down the headstone of my great-uncle, my great-grandparents, and great-great-grandparents, and Ausma digs in her big black purse for a hand trowel she has stashed there, so that she can slice a seam in the ground where begonias can bloom.

It is what I think of when Ausma and I are sitting next to each other sipping tea, reading the local paper, which features regular updates on the number of tick-infected currently bedded at the local hospital, the level of potato beetle threat, as well as an astrological chart in every issue that notes the tasks best suited to the moon's present phase.

A good day for planting annuals, reads Ausma. And manicures. And beating the rugs.

Then she turns to the jokes.

Always there are jokes on the paper's back page, usually about husbands and wives. We have taken to reading them aloud to each other in the mornings. A way to summon some light before we begin to journey into the territory of forgotten things, unspoken things, lost things.

Wife to husband reading the paper: You can stop saying, *Uh-huh, uh-huh, yea, yea, uh-uh* . . . I ended my conversation with you ten minutes ago. . . .

I move through each day a collector now of the smallest of

facts, a kind of dossier of the inconsequential, proof that I have spent long enough in Ausma's presence to have absorbed the most mundane, yet deeply human details:

She cannot sleep before it's dark.

She takes two spoons of sugar in her tea.

She prefers the radio station that plays nothing but Latvian-language pop songs, accordion-drunk polkas and hand-to-heart ballads that whisper to her in the background, a running narrative that alternates between documenting *a love like summer flowers, a love like apple blossoms,* and *women, women, oh, women who crush men's hearts, and never feel a moment's sorrow.*

At night, she places her teeth in a juice glass on a shelf above the kitchen sink, the same shelf where she keeps her only comb, and her favorite paring knife.

She has a special fondness for cats *that hold their tails like dogs.*

Her favorite tree is a birch tree that grows about a hundred meters from the house, its branches reaching low enough to rake the ground. She made a point of showing me the tree on the first day I came back to her. The tree is at least sixty years old, planted just after the war's end. She lifted the branches so that we could slip past them, and we stood for a few minutes, hidden together behind the screen of leaves. She put her palm against the burled and scarred trunk: *Look how beautifully it has grown old.*

No matter how early I try to rise, Ausma is always up before me.

Would you like new potatoes for lunch? Ausma asks. Boiled or fried? And with milk, or butter, or both?

Do you know how many times I should have died? Harijs asks. Eight times!

It doesn't matter that he has already told me; this has become like a game between us—if I don't listen, as if for the first time, he cannot be resurrected—and so over breakfast he proceeds to remind me, and himself, of all the ways he is unbreakable: the Russian soldiers he hid from in the forest when he was a boy; the mortar, years later, that went off just as far away as you are to me, and only left his ears ringing; the horse that he was riding that fell through the ice, with him still upon its back; the portion of a bridge he was helping to build that buckled and crushed his spine; the wheel of the combine that rolled over his chest, splintering ribs; the roof he tumbled from, last year, at eighty-four, snapping only a bone in his foot.

It is not so much a catalog of near-death, or a manifesto against disappearing, I decide, as a daily declaration of living: that against all odds, he is still here.

I am a cat! he says.

Go work, cat, Ausma says, flicking a dish towel in his direction, but she is smiling. The dogs need food and there's hay to get.

I have learned to wait for this moment, the table half-cleared, tea still left in her cup, and Harijs clomped-off outside.

This is when she will allow the past to enter our present space. She will tolerate my questions, sometimes even begin to share memories before I ask.

But we have an unspoken understanding that I am to let her tell the stories in any order she chooses, and when she sets down the dish towel and says, And now to work, turning her face so I can't see her tears, that means it is time to stop, that

she has offered all she can for today and now she needs time
to recover. And then she will head to the pasture where they
keep their horse, ancient, swaybacked, bristle-chinned, but
still sure-footed and true when it's time to plow their vegetable
fields. Behind her she drags a sledgehammer, which she uses
to reposition the stake that tethers the horse to the land. She
checks to see if he has bitten down all the grass the length of
his rope will allow him to reach, then she shifts him to a new
grazing spot.

After that, it will be to the shed where the chickens roost,
to collect the day's eggs from the dark corner scrimmed with
cobwebs that the hens seem to prefer. And from there, to the
currant bushes to fill a pail. Or to the edge of the garden, to
snip the withered heads from the last of the calendulas.

Time for my show, she will say when she finally comes back
inside, preempting any more possible talk between us.

She has a particular fondness for Russian and Brazilian
soap operas that have been dubbed in Latvian, and if I come
and sit next to her in the darkened room where she keeps the
old blinkering television, she will whisper the backstory to me
over the action, so that I can follow along. This woman thought
she was an orphan, but really she was the daughter of a wealthy
woman who gave her up for adoption many years ago, and
when the wealthy woman's other daughter found out, she tried
to have her half sister killed, but she only blinded her, and now,
without her sight, she fell down some steps and dropped her
baby, and it rolled into a garbage container where she couldn't
find it, and then later some strangers heard the baby crying
and thought it had been abandoned, and they couldn't have
children of their own, so they took it, and now that woman is
searching for her baby, trying to get it back.

Ausma watches, shaking her head.

How much more can a person suffer, she says.

She does not phrase it as a question.

ONCE, I THOUGHT I might see if I could take us back to the time before the present as we worked outside in the dirt.

Do any of these flowers also grow in Siberia? I asked.

For a long time, the only sound was of Ausma's spade, biting into soil, then spitting it back out.

I spent so many years trying to forget what happened in the past, she said finally. That's the only way I could keep going forward, by never returning again, not even in my memories.

We dug on in silence.

What I did not see then that I can see now: that there are many ways to make a declaration, without ever uttering a word.

The weight of cherries falling in a pail, the milky heat of a kitten's breath, the dusted outline of the gelding's ribs as it huffs happily into its hay, the sound of Harijs whistling from the barn as he repairs the horse's tack—this sweet simple life, focused on the present, this was Ausma's way of saying, *Here is how I have survived. Here is how I live—so that I am able to live.*

I still don't know what it says about me that even after this became clear, I kept asking Ausma to go back into the time before the present.

That she kept going back into the time before the present says everything about her love for me.

And Harijs's repeated recitations of calamity, always in the moments leading up to my morning conversation with Ausma,

I have come to suspect that I misunderstood completely what he intended with that ritual.

That maybe all along, what he had been trying to do, over and over again, with all the life that remained in him, was to offer me his trauma, so that he might spare his love from talking about hers.

VI

I T WAS MARCH, the month when vipers sometimes rained from the sky, dropped onto unsuspecting heads by storks, clumsy-beaked, languorous-winged, scaly legs dragging through the low clouds. If it were possible for us to rise up high enough to join them on their lazed glide across the land, to look down upon it from their point of view, this is what we might have seen on that day, at the beginning of the spring that would mark the end of her former life. Below us, the fields, stubbled and brooding, like a man slowly lifting his head from the table to see so many empty bottles. And now the roof of the schoolhouse that had been raised from red stone, and where, inside, some children were still forgetting at the top of their school compositions to record the date as 1949, not 1948. There, perhaps a dog, sitting at the edge of a driveway, one hind leg hoisted toward the sky to make room for its rooting snout, guard to what once would have been called a house, but was now nothing more than the hollowed-out testimony of a mistimed machine-gun strafing. On that day, five years before, a Russian plane had swooped low, aiming for the German troops retreating on the nearby road, but all that fell in the plane's wake was a horse, a woman and, finally, the old farmhouse, where the woman had planned to give birth to the child who died with her. But now, this day, upon that same road: a girl. Boots stamping mud, in one version of her memories. Bicycle wheels churning beneath her, in another. Either way: sent off that morning by her mother, pinch-browed, dim-eyed, drained by the effort of trying to still the worry humming inside her, like a wasp trapped between windowpanes: *Why don't you go to town, child, bring this fabric to the seamstress and let her measure you for a dress.* She took what her mother pressed on her, said nothing.

She knew what her mother really meant: that maybe in town, she might hear some news about her brother. He had driven off from their farm a day before to see about a gelding. It was long past the time he should have been back.

And so Ausma went, out the door of the farmhouse, past the sign into which its name was carved, *Lembi*, and headed in the direction of the sun. On a good day, the walk to town took two hours, a chance to catalog the things that had returned with winter's ouster, the first new thrusts of grass, as pale and awkward as colts' legs; the skitter of birds' claws on green wood, and then, maybe, the high pealing bawls of a kinglet, or the dizzy, gulping chants of a warbler—whoever had ridden the winds back north first.

A truck passed, trailing a spray of mud, but otherwise it seemed as if she had the road to herself. What she could not see: her family's farmhouse, some distance behind her already, and the truck rolling to a stop in front. And off in the distance ahead of her: the village, with its houses and churches and businesses, the distillery, the abattoir, the candy factory that made caramels wrapped with portraits of voluptuous cows, hock-deep in clover. And just beyond all that: the town's railroad tracks, where, for the last twenty-four hours, cattle cars had been coupled and locked into place, one after another, until they formed a great snaking line, so long that it did not end, just dissolved into the horizon. And on either side of the tracks, piles of boards, those that were not needed by the men who, while the rest of the village slept, had hammered them against the car walls to form crude bunk beds and over the windows so that no one could see, the sound of the driving nails like the churring of so many nightjars.

The town revealed to her nothing of this, and later, upon reflection, everything. It was the tiniest of tells: her hand raised in greeting to a man she thought she knew; the man dropping his head, so she saw only his hat. At the time she told herself maybe she'd confused him for someone else.

Not a sign of her brother anywhere. In the seamstress's shop: the sound of needles punching through fabric, steady and methodical. And then all that was left was to go back home.

At first, she couldn't understand what she was seeing as she approached the farmhouse: the front door, extended wide like the mouth of a yawning cat.

Then she felt the shards of broken crockery snapping underfoot.

VII

NOT MANY people seem to remember anymore, but the living used to sing as a way to reach the dead, to make the dead heard in this world.

> *I spend my days in a house made of wood,*
> *Above me spans a roof of green.*
> *I have never opened the doors to this house,*
> *Never opened my eyes to the sun.*

The living would sing in the voices of the dead:

> *Give me please, my dear little god,*
> *Some land of my own.*
> *I don't need much.*
> *Something as wide as the length of a man's forearm,*
> *As deep as a man is tall.*

And sometimes, the dead would sound a little maudlin, as if they, too, had just polished off a bottle of vodka, soft-lipped, eyes wet like the inside of the shot glasses scattered across the table:

I sleep deeply, sweetly,
Steps from the endless sea.
The waters sing, the stones weep.
The distant swells sparkle.

Other times, the dead showed a testy side, roaring like a drunk the next morning, woken by little more than the padding of cat paws across his pillow:

What is all this snorting, all this howling
Right next to my grave?

And the living would have to cross back over to their side, in order to answer the dead:

That's not snorting, that's not howling.
That's just your relatives mourning.

Enough of this sorrow, the dead tried to insist. But it sounded hollow and unconvincing, channeled through the lips of the living. Sorrow was always embedding itself in the experiences of the living,

like a bee trying to make a hive in a splintery oak.

Like a nail hidden in the grass; his bare foot treading upon its tip; the churning of his jaw, the arching of his back, the way he rises up off the bed, pinned to the mattress only by his heels and the crown of his head; the stillness that follows; the letters he wrote, *Dear Livija*, tied off with a ribbon, placed deep in a drawer; the sound a drawer makes as a hand scrapes it closed.

> *Come my love, my fiancé,*
> *Come see where I sleep beneath a hill of sand.*

It's a train door opening onto an endless, whipping cold, a bundle released, and then nothing but a guard's empty hands.

> *What happened to the white snows?*
> *What happened to my beautiful body?*
> *Sun ate the white snows.*
> *Earth ate my body.*

WE HAVE NO SONGS to reach my grandmother, Livija, only the lilt and drift of Ausma's memories of her sister, which I collect, and then pocket, like they are so many perfect stones.

I ask: What was she like when she when she was younger?

And Ausma answers:

Well, you have to remember, she was fourteen when I was born. To me she was very glamorous. Always perfectly dressed. Always looking in the mirror. She had many boys who liked her, before your grandfather, but one who was very special. She kept his letters in her room, and I snuck them out once, intending to read them, but after just a few sentences, I felt ashamed for taking them. They were too private, words no one else but the two of them should know. I used to get all her cast-off clothes, which were beautiful, because she was, but I didn't like that I never got anything new. I do remember she had a big black coat, with a ruff of fur at the throat. She wore it when I went to visit her in Riga once, before the war. At the time, I dreamed of being grown-up enough one day to wear that coat, too. *Ha!* That seems so funny to me now. And a hat with a feather that swooped like this.

I nod. She somehow managed to look elegant just going to the supermarket, or hanging laundry, I say.

Livija did everything just so, says Ausma. Her stitches were always straight. Her dough, always soft and light, like so many feathers! I looked up to her. Our mother was sick a lot of the time, especially after I was born, so Livija raised me, really—a surrogate mother. Like she raised you. She was the one who braided my hair. She was the one who fed me. She was the one who taught me how to knit and how to read, before I even started school. But oh, she was a demanding teacher. She made me sit and work for hours. Stop fidgeting, she would say. Practice your letters!

How old were you when you last saw her, before she went away? I ask.

Let's see, says Ausma, it was the last time she came to visit the farm. She had just married your grandfather and they had just had their first baby. I was fourteen, I think. Yes, that's right. I was fourteen. Maybe I was fifteen. But no older. Oh how I missed her all the way in Riga. And then the phones stopped working. And then the trains. And then she was gone.

When did you hear from her again?

Not until we had come back from Siberia. By then, she was in America.

So neither of you knew what happened to the other after the war?

No, Ausma says. Not even during the war. She was in Riga.

We were here. Hiding in the forest with the cows as the planes dropped bombs. What we each lived through, we lived through alone. Without the other ever feeling along.

I FEEL *along with you*, the Latvians say, when they want to express genuine understanding, compassion, even sympathy toward one another. It's interesting to me the way the construction of the phrase implies action, movement.

As if any true act of empathy demands not only emotional projection but also physical accompaniment, a willingness to travel with the other, deep into the unknown of wherever it is they must go.

PLEASE, AUSMA SAID, Take me, too.

She said it standing on the platform, crying and arguing with the soldiers who stood guard over the row of boxcars that stretched down the tracks. Through the gaps she could see eyes blinking, hands snatching at the air. Letters dropped to the tracks, and the people in the boxcars yelled to those who stood outside: Please pick up my note and bring it to my relatives, let them know where I am.

Upon discovering the ransacked farmhouse, Ausma had run to her father's cousin's farm.

Your mother and brother are at the train station, her cousin's husband told her, and he took her there, led her to the car that held them.

Her mother cried and reached to her through the opening. I'm glad you're safe, she said, and Ausma realized that her mother must have suspected something, sent her away on an errand to the seamstress on purpose, so she was not at home when the soldiers arrived.

Ausma cupped water in her hands, brought what she could to her mother's and brother's mouths. They told her they had heard the railcars were scheduled to depart the next morning, and although no one would tell them where they were headed, everyone knew, because it was not the first time.

What will you do? they asked her.

She didn't know what to say.

That night, at her cousin's, she tried to think.

They let her cry for her family, and then they told her to be practical.

You can't do anything for them now. Best to save yourself. You are young. You still have a chance. That's how you can help them now: by making sure someone lives.

That's what she would remember, years later:

Make sure someone lives.

She didn't sleep, and left in the morning before the sun. She would need supplies for the journey ahead, and she hoped to make it back to the farmhouse before a new wave of looters arrived.

A woolen blanket, a small hatchet, a honey tin. That was all the house had left to give her.

They tried to turn her away at the train station. The soldiers told her she was a stupid girl. Go home, they said. They could not understand what she was trying to do. Who volunteered for their own exile?

But she begged, and she pleaded—*take me too*—and finally they agreed to unlock the door of the railcar where her mother and brother were held.

Ausma stepped into the dark.

It's me, she said, because they couldn't see who it was at first. I'm coming with you.

You're here? My girl is here? her mother cried. Oh, what are you doing, she said, her voice caught somewhere between relief and grief. What are you doing.

And now I come intruding from the present to ask how old she was when she gave herself up.

She says, I was sixteen.

But later, as I am running through the dates, I realize that this cannot be right, that she would have been twenty-one when she stood on the railway platform and asked to be sent with her family to Siberia.

I mention this to Ausma. She looks at me for a long time.

I was sixteen when my life ended, she says again.

I try once more: But that's before Siberia.

Yes, she says. But that's why it wasn't so hard for me to go. I felt like my life was already over.

At sixteen?

She nods.

What happened when you were sixteen?

She doesn't answer.

Ausma?

VIII

THE LATVIANS have always named their farms, as if they were living things, and it is a name that tends to remain— still printed on all official maps, like the one I am holding now, unfurled on the backseat, pinned against the wind roaring in through the open windows with my fingertips—long after all other evidence of that farm has disappeared.

Whether out of respect or neglect or superstition or maybe all three, when a farmhouse is abandoned in the countryside, it is never torn down. It's left just as it was the moment the last person pulled the door closed. And in this way it will sit—as rain tongues plaster from the walls, as the weight of the winter snow snaps ceiling joists—waiting for someone to return.

Sometimes, though, this waiting goes on for so long that the farm can no longer remember what it once was. Like a drunk counting backwards, it is unable to retrace the exact order of its unmaking. And yet, maybe that is not such a bad thing.

Because watch what happens as each shingle scattered on the ground lifts, drifting back onto the roof.

See walls unbuckle, the center beam unsplinter.

Brick by brick, the chimney rises. Vines retreat. Windows unshatter.

And now boards must mend to restore the edge of the hayloft upon which suddenly my great-grandfather alights, as if spit from somewhere far below, feet scrabbling, neck untwisting, a death repeated, even as it is reversed.

AUSMA IS THE ONE who finally suggests that we visit together. We've been circling the subject for weeks, and I have been hesitant to push her. I have been eager to visit whatever remains, to register the progress of the farm's decay over the past year, but it's too far to walk on my own.

I haven't been back to Lembi for so long, Ausma says, her belly to the sink, using the blunt side of a knife to scrape the skins off potatoes that she's just spaded from the soil. I don't want to see it anymore. There's nothing there, anyway. Why would you want to go there?

It seemed like the happiest place my grandmother had ever known, I say. She talked about it with me so much, it seemed like she wanted me to know it, the way she knew it.

Ausma studies me.

The farm was a very different place for my sister, she says. She could enjoy her youth there.

And you? I ask.

It took my childhood, she says.

Then, suddenly, one morning, over tea and tomatoes and pickled herring, Ausma announces that this would be the perfect day to take a drive.

The hay can wait, she says to Harijs, who has spent the last week winching half-ton rolls of hay into the loft of the old cowshed. Get the car.

With Harijs at the wheel, we lurch onto the main road, past Ausma's old horse rubbing against the bark of an oak tree, past the storks, trailing a few steps behind the harvesting tractors, beaks open for prey scattered by the blades. I move to put my seat belt on and Ausma laughs. There's no point out here, she says, and it's not clear whether she means that the gesture is unnecessary, or that it's futile. I let go of the strap.

Soon it is only dirt beneath the tires. Ausma names the abandoned farms we pass. That belonged to my godfather, she says. He disappeared in the war. No body. We never knew what happened to him. There—our neighbors. Dead.

As she speaks, stands of birch and ash and aspen rise and repeat, a white noise that drowns out all other landmarks, yet somehow Ausma can still sense when we have crossed the old property line.

This is where Lembi starts, she announces over the droning of the trees. Right here.

Right here, the baron's secretary said. Sign here.

And my great-great-grandfather, who never learned to write his own name, drew three "X"s.

It is the eighth of January 1882, and with those quill strokes Andrejs Smits is the first of his family to own the land where his ancestors before him have lived and worked and died.

Their home has always belonged to someone else. Going all the way back to the days of mud and sticks and squatting forms huddled in marshes, honing bone with sharpened stones, the region's inhabitants have only ever really held the briefest of claims to the ground that they lived upon, or had a say in what it is called, or how it will appear on any maps.

Babies here might be born under the flag of one nation, but by the time they draw their next breath, another flag is already being unfurled.

Where do you come from?

Always, there are two possible answers:

I come from —— [insert name of country today].

Or: I come from here.

Here—meaning the grass and stones beneath a person's feet, the ground upon which they are raised. Because that will never change, regardless of who happens to be ruling at any particular moment.

Here pins each person to something solid against which they can always reference themselves, no matter how weird or confusing things get, the way a drunk puts his toes on the floor beside the bed to try to stop the swirls.

And for its part, each successive occupation also sees those who live in these territories as inseparable from their land—as in: desirable features of a particular property, tallied on plat maps like water sources, hillocks or meadows.

But there is no concept of the Latvians as a people, except in relation to what they can do for others, because there is no concept of Latvia as a country, except in relation to what it can provide to others.

To be born in the territories now known as Latvia prior to the twentieth century is to more than likely be born a serf, bound under hereditary contract to provide a lifetime of labor to the wealthy friends of whatever empire happens to be ruling at the time. In the three or so centuries leading up to my great-great-grandfather's purchase, the countryside is largely under the possession of titled Germans, some of them descendants of the Brothers of the Sword who helped the Catholic Church tame the region's pagan tribes.

They have last names like von Wolf or von Hen, sons and daughters of men named Johan Gottlieb II or Heinrich Johan I—friends, counsel and cousins to the tsars. They refer to the

Latvians as a whole as *not-German*. Alongside the Latvians' crops, they raise neo-Gothic manors and neo-Romanesque manors, baroque manors, manors with Corinthian columns that support carved pediments of birds and flowers and family crests through which they usher their opera-singer brides, their Italian-novelist lovers.

They build stables and riding arenas and wine cellars and plant shrubs in the shape of their spouses' initials, pour concrete for platforms upon which they may enjoy afternoon tea as they look out over their lands. There is no limit to their wealth, but, out here in the countryside, they discover there is a limit to their knowledge.

They do not know how to handle rye seed, how to lay by hand the stone foundations of a livestock barn. They cannot gauge by the change in the light when it is time to head to the fields with the scythes, have never burned the bedding and clothing of the dead and then turned the warm ashes back into the soil.

For the care and cultivation of those things that exist beyond the baron's understanding, he turns to his serfs—like the family of my great-great-grandfather—happy to prosper from their knowledge, even if he is not certain it qualifies as a form of intelligence.

These are people, after all, who insist on the existence of devils, so say the pastors hired by the barons to run the local churches. They have heard the farmers talking, heard them speaking to one another about visitations and sightings, though how much of what is being said can the German-speaking pastors truly catch? There exists no written version of their parishioners' language to refer to, except for what the clergy themselves begin to try to create from the Latvians' chatter.

But the sounds keep slipping just beyond the pastors' reach. Shh, one hears. Tsch, hears another. At one point, there are a dozen proposed variations of just one letter. It's possible to listen, but never hear. The serfs understand perfectly, though, when one says to another:

If you wake in the morning to find a devil has left footprints in your field, wait for the next rain. Then drink the water caught in his tread.

Or a man says:

Once, the devil surprised me after I had fallen asleep while working in the threshing barn. "Who's that in there?" the devil asked. "Linen," I said. The devil wanted to know if he could come in, too. "Only if you can endure everything I have had to endure," I said. "And what have you had to endure?" the devil wanted to know. So I told him: "Along with hundreds of others, I have tried to make a life from the soil, but then one day, we were set upon, yanked from our home, and our heads chopped off. Then we were drowned in water, and left to bake in the sun. After that, all our bones were broken, what was left of our bodies pulverized. Finally, we were combed and spun and then threaded through needles, woven and then sewn and then worn and then used until we were nothing but brittle rags." But by the time I had finished recounting all this, the devil had decided he couldn't in fact endure all this, not even as a story, and he fled.

When one of the barons unveils on his property a gate through which all guests must pass and names it Devil's Gate, it's hard to know whether this is meant to be a pointed reference of self-awareness or a simplistic attempt to mock local super-stition. Regardless, the baron staffs Devil's Gate with men who it is said as a condition of their employment must never bathe or change their clothes or cut their hair, so as to look like wretched beings of the other-world, gnashing and howling for the passing carriages, then presumably heading back to their room inside the gatehouse to warm a cup of brackish tea.

Beyond Devil's Gate lies the castle with battlements and stone lions and a pond that wishes it was a moat. It has been in the possession of the von Tranze family since the early 1800s. From the exposed-timber beams they hang chandeliers in the shape of mermaids, forever gliding through the air in the direction of their finely cusped breasts. The von Tranzes love, too, the empty armor of dead knights, lavish arrange-ments of flowers and feathers that spill from vases sculpted to look like gliding swans. They collect wall-size paintings of capering fauns, barrel-loined centaurs—anything by the artist Hans Makart, darling of nineteenth-century Viennese society, lover of allegory and thick gold leaf, inspiration to Gustav Klimt.

This is where the peasants come when they must seek the baron's favor. As a people they are not unaccustomed to the idea that the everyday world can be populated with the fan-tastical, recognizing as they do not only the very real possi-bility of devils in their midst, but also cats possessed with the hidden power of speech, weddings which take place between the sun and the moon, gods concealed in tassels of wheat. Still, what must they make of all these translucent-skinned nymphs and scepter-wielding Dianas, all the wolves and lions that emerge from their dens carved deep in the wooden lintels to listen, teeth exposed, as the serfs plead their requests. Maybe you were caught stealing wood from the baron's forest and so the overseer took your saw. Or maybe you have found a girl and you are ready to exchange wedding rings—iron bands fashioned from blacksmiths' scraps—but before you and your bride can say it for yourselves, the baron must first say yes.

The grandmothers say that if you slap the jamb of the door on your way in, it might ensure that the baron's resistance lasts only as long as the sound of your palm against the wood.

What they mean: Go ahead and ask. But you can't expect to hold any more sway than a simple knock of flesh against wood.

Those same grandmothers will also tell you: A stone often lifted never becomes green.

What they mean: Don't hope too much. Best to accept your situation, endure.

This is what qualifies among the serfs as happy talk. The Germans for their part find the Latvians to be terrifyingly grim, stoic to the point of catatonia. About fifty years before my great-great-grandfather's birth, a book circulates among the landed class, a chronicle of Latvian peasant life written by the son of a rural minister who hopes that his grim, unblinking account of serf existence will guilt landowners into repentance and reform.

A Latvian reacts to the suffering and death of his children or his closest relatives with an unsettling blank calm. No one has ever shown him any empathy, and so he cannot summon it when it comes to others. Given the crushing grip of his everyday wants, all ties, even those between blood relatives, are as fragile as a spider's web. In their lives, we see the effects of constant, sustained cruelty.

Soon it is all anyone is reading. On fainting couches stuffed with horse's hair, or from the pillowed nests of four-poster beds. Editions are ordered in Russian and French and Danish. Some people read it with the kind of heavy shame that one reserves for Martin Luther's version of church, rough stone under bare knees. But others read it hungrily, compulsively, skipping the more pedestrian sections on Latvian folklore and language to get right to the shocking bits.

If there happened to be a smallpox outbreak, mothers would take their unweaned infants to the homes of the infected, so that the baby would catch the disease. Or the mother would smear pus from the smallpox on bread with butter and feed it to her children. When challenged, the mother simply replies, "Better for the child to die now, if he is going to die than to eat all our bread and then die."

Even as the barons publicly denounce the book as little more than incendiary propaganda to stoke sympathy for the serfs, even as they engineer the expulsion of its writer from Latvia, many still keep copies of *The Latvians* on their library shelves for those times when they require a reference to the more confounding aspects of their workers' psychologies. And so long before my great-great-grandfather is conceived, he is already created, the fundamental elements of his character loosed in the fanning of these pages, thousands of gloved fingers tracing the black and white lines that will split, then replicate, the raw code of his inheritance:

The strangest unfortunates

eternally changeable

Semiliterate folk

*yet one of the richest spoken languages in terms of
perceptive and picturesque words*

superstitious

primitive

Born to be domestic beasts

Through the blood and mucus, my great-great-grandfather takes his first gasp of air, mouth working like one of the carp rising to the surface of the manor's moat. He is technically the first in his family to breathe freely—while he has been floating in his mother's belly, the barons, under mounting calls for reform, have torn up all the peasants' hereditary obligations, effectively emancipating all serfs—and yet my great-great-grandfather is born as much under the control of the barons as his ancestors ever were. Because while the barons' gesture has saved the serfs from a lifetime of required service, it has also effectively separated the serf from his farm. Under the old system, serfs might be a baron's property and receive no real pay, but in return, it was understood that the serf would live upon the land where he had always lived. He could count on baron's equipment and his support in order to do that, because while the arrangement allowed the serfs to keep a little back for themselves, enough to survive, it was in the baron's interest, too, because he stood to gain from whatever extra they might grow.

Now all land belongs exclusively to the barons, and the barons are free to choose who will be the land's tenants going forward. They can charge rent—and set the terms as high as they like. They are under no obligation to give anyone the chance to stay.

So this is what freedom brings: a surname, but little else. Maybe your last name is assigned by the baron, his final attempt to leave a mark on what was his property. Or maybe it is written down by one of the parish scribes, sent from farmhouse to farmhouse to try to create a census of the newly emancipated, so that they can be taxed, their sons conscripted. Hovering at the threshold of all those darkened rooms, eyes burning with wood smoke, the smell of cow, dirt trapped beneath hooves, drying herbs:

And what will you call yourself now?

Think.

Little stone.

Plowman.

Birch grove.

Sparrow.

Swell of earth.

If you take too long, and he is tired, the scribe might just assign you something, anything, gleaned from a single wincing glimpse into the darkness:

Keg drainer.

Earthworm.

Dog head.

Lady bits.

Or perhaps, if he has exhausted all other possibilities, and can think of nothing else:

Schmid, German for Smith, which when written with the Latvian alphabet is Smits.

This will be the name my great-great-grandfather carries forward for us, a name he can say but cannot write. Neutral, impassive, name as placeholder, worn into the coming hunger years, the years of revolt and flight.

No one is required to work for the barons anymore, but then again, no one is allowed to move beyond the boundaries of the parish where they were born, so that the barons don't lose their workforce. The land that once kept them now traps them. Many find themselves right back at the barons' estates, begging for work as paid laborers. But they find that what little they make does not support them as well as the food that came from the ground they were allowed to live upon as serfs. Even those who manage to come to terms with the barons, who are renting back farmland from them, are discovering how this new life can bring just as much suffering as serfdom ever did, with no one to help them with equipment—unless they rent it from the barons, and fall further into debt, no one to underwrite the crops, no one to absorb the cost of seeds that fail, animals that falter, rain that doesn't come.

They are starving.

My great-great-grandfather among them.

He digs in, trying to learn how to live under the new terms, fields that go unsown without the baron's patronage, except for the ribs and the pinbones of downed milk cattle, weeds growing through desiccated hides.

This how the dreams of leaving begin.

They sing of it first in their songs, the songs they give one another in the place of written words, the stories they tell themselves about themselves, spilling from one mouth to another, open, hungry:

> *Oh where can I flee, little god of mine?*
> *These woods are full of wolves and bears*
> *These fields are full of tyrants*

Rumor finally supplies a destination: more than three thousand kilometers to the south, along the shores of the Black Sea, land is said to be free for the taking, the soil so rich the smallest fruits, currants, cherries, grow the size of a fat sow's shoats.

Thousands begin to imagine their exodus, what they will pack, which horse will carry them to their new home. They even change their faith in preparation. Over three frantic years, forty thousand peasants pledge themselves to the Russian Orthodox Church. Golden onion domes sprout across the countryside.

But this will be the closest any of them ever come to realizing their Black Sea fantasies: standing once a week in the pew-less nave, hay-tangled hair perfumed by incense, the air around them turned to chanting, endless, repeating, like the lap of waves against a faraway shore. Yet even as this particular relocation fantasy will not prove viable, it has taught the peasants how to imagine leaving, that leaving is a possibility actually available to them. So when the decision finally comes to grant peasants the freedom to move beyond their parish, thousands go as far as they are able, off to the capital, weary of practicing flight only in their imaginations—the first subjects in what will prove to be a long-term test: what becomes of the former serf when he is separated from his countryside.

But still more decide not to go anywhere at all, as if watch-

ing all this leave-taking has made them that much more determined to try to stay, even when staying seems impossible. This
is what my great-great-grandfather chooses. To remain a stone
never lifted. He waits. And he waits. Quietly, in one place. A
wife comes to him. Then a son. The winters shorten and the
summers lengthen. He can save some grain. The sheep do not
starve. The cows no longer sow the fields with their bones. He
slips the animals from their skins, tans their hides into leather,
turns the leather into shoes, which he sells to the baron. He
collects the coins, feels the weight pull his pockets toward the
ground. So that when the baron finally announces he is willing
to sell land to his workers, quick as the rap of a shoe-blackened
palm against the doorjamb, my great-great-grandfather comes
to the castle to ask whether he might have a chance to buy the
property upon which his family has lived.

The baron says yes—for 4238 rubles. Of course, he would
be willing to extend credit.

My great-great-grandfather, quill ready, offers his reply:

XXX.

And with that, the land known as Lembi, once the property of the von Tranze family, becomes his.

THIS IS THE ROOM where your grandmother was born. This
is the room where I was born. This is the room where our
brother slept when he came home from the labor camp, after
the war, no leg, so weak, there, where the weeds are coming
through that opening—that was once a window. This is where
our mother slept by herself after it happened, her bed here in

the corner. And this is where she was sitting when the soldiers came, when they told her to get her things, come with them. They didn't even bother to close the front door, just left it open so the cats would run inside.

Ausma dips her head to avoid a root that has punctured the softening ceiling, and briefly suspends her narrative.

Harijs had driven us in the old car as far as the brush and rutted fields would allow, and Ausma and I had gone the rest of the way on foot, deep into the tick-thick stands of grass, cow parsley, wild caraway, hogweed. We moved slowly. The grasses, dried now by the long summer's sun, nipped at our arms, our legs, our necks, leaving long weeping welts.

I don't know what could possibly be left for us to see here anymore—not after so much time has passed, Ausma had said as we began our slow plow from the car.

Now we are stepping on shingles that snap underfoot, scattered two-by-fours that throw us off balance and cause our ankles to bow.

Slowly, a roof rises above the grass line to meet us, though its edges sag, brushing the ground in places, like the hem of a skirt coming loose. Here and there, sections of standing wood try to hold the shape of an exterior wall, but so many boards have tired and pulled away that the unbroken stretches begin to unnerve me, perhaps because they serve as a reminder that once there had been something on the other side. The house has decayed significantly in just the last year, since I first visited.

Through the gaps I see the outlines of empty rooms, as uncertain and hesitant as if drawn by someone trying to map the interior of a childhood home, unrecalled for decades. My eye is drawn to the ragged hole where a window should be, a sudden movement there—and even though I realize it is simply the yellowing edge of a curtain, twitching, this feels more unsettling, obscene even, than anything else I could have imagined.

Next to me, Ausma moans. Oh you are so horrible now, she says. She is speaking directly to the collapsing structure in front of us. I don't even recognize you.

I wonder if I have made a mistake, letting her come here, if it might not be too much for her, and I'm about to suggest that we can head back to the car now and home, that I can try to find a way to return one day on my own, when I realize she is moving again, walking ahead of me, tracing the perimeter of the structure one limping step at a time, trying to reacquaint herself with what remains: Here was the front door, the little porch. And I can see that the door she is pointing to hangs slightly ajar, far enough from its frame that I might be able to hook my fingers around it and pull.

I look at her. She holds my eyes.

I take this as agreement. I step over a pane of unbroken glass, slide my hand behind the splintering wood, and heave.

The smell rises up to meet me first, earth unturned, but for the claws of mice, hundreds of them, working undisturbed for years, the bitter stink of mold, unrinsed beer bottles left in a corner by someone who must have crawled back here at some point to drink and piss himself in the unseeing dark, thinking no one would ever know.

I'm inside before I realize it, before I have even turned to ask Ausma if she thinks it a good idea. But by the time I stop and turn back to the doorway, she is already slipping through the opening behind me, tugging her skirt away from the jutting nails.

We move cautiously, flushing rats from mounds of debris with each step. They skitter ahead of us, tails thrashing. In many rooms, the support beams have buckled, demanding that we crouch in order to pass. Metal scavengers have broken in at some point; stubs of electrical wiring protrude from the walls and ceilings where the thieves have managed to rip out lines by hand. Where wallpaper remains, it hangs in ragged sheets.

This is where we ate our meals, Ausma says. She has been reclaiming each broken room we enter, trying to return it to the way it was. Right here, this is where I saw your grandmother for the very last time. She is addressing me now, but it still feels as though she is also directing her words to the house itself, to a presence that emerges only when she is here.

We walk from room to room, so long that I begin to realize how dangerous this really is, the roots clawing their way through the floor, the softening spots that give way beneath my feet, the angry strip of ceiling hanging above us, shock-white, black-stained with rain, like the inside of a scalp peeled back from the skull.

This is where we laid his body out, Ausma is saying, here, in this room, in that corner, there. Livija had already disappeared by then. We didn't know where she was. We buried him without her.

The floor creaks beneath our weight, little songs of grief, as if it is also remembering that day, the voices of the mourners.

> We are to die, we are to rot.
> But our name is to stay here,
> Our name is to stay here,
> In this corner of the room.

Janis. That's the name his wife screamed, kept screaming, after she found him, neck twisted on the floor of the barn.

Janis and Ausma. Those are the names he had been calling, less than an hour before, summoning his son and daughter to him. Here, take the wagon and deliver this grain for me to the farmer up the road who helped with our harvest.

His voice was warm, riffled from drink. His cousin had shown up that morning, despondent over a woman. Janis had taken one look at the man, then pulled two glasses from the shelf and uncorked a bottle.

It was afternoon now and the day was getting away from them, and so he had decided to delegate, send his two children to make the delivery, while he quickly climbed into the loft to get some hay so his wife could feed the cows. Then they could open a new bottle and go back to solving the problems of the heart.

It was an accident. A miscalculation. He did not realize how close he was standing to the loft's lip. A misstep, a wobble. He tried to set a boot down to steady himself, and stepped back into air.

Ausma would swear later it was ravens that told her first, circling in the sky overhead as she and her brother drove the horse and wagon in the direction of home.

> *The raven ran into the skies, dripping gore.*
> *Quick, grab a broom made of linden branches.*
> *Brush away the drops of blood*
> *The raven has left.*

And that is one kind of telling.
Here is another:

A neighbor racing to the edge of the road, shouting to the figures on the wagon, telling them to hurry home, to Lembi.

That was the name she called out.

Not my great-grandfather's name. But the name of the farm.

IX

THAT NIGHT, back at Ausma's house, we eat in silence.

Ausma nibbles at her slice of brown bread, pushes a potato around her plate with the back of her fork, the tin tips of its tines chiming softly in protest.

Finally, she speaks. I haven't talked about the day he died, since it happened, she says. And now I can't stop thinking about it, seeing him again in my mind, his neck. Her voice catches.

Harijs looks at her for a long time, then at me.

Did you know my father once danced with a bear? he asks.

Ausma sets down her fork, pushes back from the table. We watch as she slippers off toward her room. The door latches. Then there is the unmistakable sound of crying.

Harijs presses on.

He was walking in the forest one day, and he surprised the bear. The bear reared up, like this—Harijs rises off his stool to full height, waggles his trap-sized hands like claws—and my father knew he didn't have time to run, if he turned his back he'd surely be dead. So he made himself as big as he could and rushed straight at the bear, with all his strength, with his arms out wide, as if to clasp a bride. And—*bang*, Harijs smashes the meat of his palms together—he and the bear, they met, chest to chest. My father held on tight to the bear's middle, and the bear held tight to him. Like this, each standing on two legs, they danced.

How did it end? I ask, although I realize as soon as the words are out of my mouth that *how* is never the question that drives the telling of any anecdote in Latvia. What matters, as with all stories here, is the unspoken *why*.

The bear, it clung to his shoulder. And locked together like this, they turned around and around, until *shrick*—Harijs rakes the air with one of his claw-hands—the bear managed to draw a paw across my father's back. But my father didn't let go. He said some words to the bear, right into its ear, and for whatever reason, the bear finally stopped. It dropped down to all fours and it looked in his eyes one last time. Then it turned, and it ran. Who knows why. Maybe—and here Harijs meets my eyes—it was tired of dancing.

At this, Harijs rises and shuffles down the hall to Ausma's room.

I can hear him rapping gently with his big hands, then calling to her, his cheek to the door, the stubbled skin of it tracing the wood like sandpaper.

Don't cry, my love, he whispers, his own voice breaking.

NOT QUITE ten years after my great-great-grandfather signs the deed to Lembi and becomes the owner of its land, as one century begins to slip into the next, a poem is published in Latvian.

The poem's author is a man, magnificently whiskered, with a beard that bristles like a pine's needles. Beneath it, he wears a face that looks as if it has been summoned from a series of precise angles, like the view through a surveyor's transit—an instrument he has spent a good percentage of his adult life carrying through the countryside east of Riga, taking exact measure of the land and its people, noting the new farmsteads that are emerging, now freed from the old outlines of the baron's estates, making the once invisible borders of the peasants' presence here something definite in the world.

He knows the peasants' stories. The words to the secret histories they convey to each other when they sing to one another, the way others learn by reading books. He understands because he himself comes from a family of farmers who worked as tenants on an estate.

And although he is part of the first generation that is born free, able, in theory, to choose any life now, not just the life of a serf, he finds there are still limits on what he can hope for himself. He is picked by his local parish priests as one of just three peasants' children to study for the first time for free at one of the church schools where the barons and other well-to-do residents normally send their offspring. Where all the subjects are taught in German. And although he excels in school, the top student in his class after three years, his family doesn't have the money for him to pursue further study, and when he goes back to the priests to appeal for help, he is pushed to forget his academic dreams, to focus instead on making his living as a laborer.

And so he labors. He helps his father manage the properties of a series of manors, turns wood in the winters as a carpenter. He finds work as a ferryman, floating people across the river Daugava, dragging his pole through its silty waters, watching his changing reflection dart and shiver, like the fish that trail in the raft's wake.

He is in his midtwenties when he finally becomes a surveyor's assistant, his pockets lined with levels and rulers. And also: pens. Because ideas are coming to him, clipped, precise lines of poetry, arranged like the grids of his emerging maps.

Even as he sets the boundaries of the existing world, he can see the invisible one that fits inside of it, the hidden inhabitants and phenomena and cultural landmarks that appear whenever they are given voice, whether spoken or sung.

He uses these old ideas to craft new lines of verse, jots them in the margins of his field notes, next to his calculations. And he senses that this could be the beginning of something more sustained, an epic even.

But first, he must live his own version of the epic, the restlessness, followed by a requisite period of wandering, of fortune seeking, of testing one's self against the challenges that come only through a period of self-imposed exile.

His self-imposed exile leads him to Moscow, where he falls in with a circle of journalists and intellectuals whose thoughts on nationalism will ultimately spur him to volunteer as a surveyor for the Russian army, so that he might help the Serbs battle for independence against the Ottoman Empire.

The military offers mobility. A spot at officers' training school. And then, finally, a commission that delivers him back home, to the land where he grew up, this time in uniform, medals clinking.

Upon his return, Andrejs Pumpurs begins to compose a series of cantos that flow from him, a strange liquid rilling of time. Chants, he calls them.

It's as if he has set himself back upon the river he once worked as a ferryman, his thoughts drifting like the old raft he rowed from shore to shore, his subconscious sending to the surface everything he has ever read or heard or seen.

Bobbing by him now: a waterlogged copy of *The Chronicle of Henry of Livonia*, penned by a priest from the thirteenth century who witnessed firsthand the work of the knights of the Brothers of the Sword, as they attempted to tame Europe's last pagans, a document of the violence required to subdue these people, who too long had been living, in the words of Pope Innocent III, *in the darkness of infidelity*, with their animal offerings and their queer way of thinking, which, with His divine help, would now finally vanish: eclipses said to be the auguries of an angry god who has used his teeth to gnaw away the sun; forests that mean more than the life of any man, trees which no axe must ever touch; *hills* and *valleys* and *cliffs* and *caves* and *plants* and *beasts* and *impure spirits* that are spoken to like sacred things by people who prefer *to serve the created rather than the Creator.*

The poet fishes the priest's book from the flow of his memories, shakes its soggy pages, then turns it upside down.

The old gods float past, Thunder, Mother Fate, the Daughters of the Sun.

Then come witches, hissing and spitting, lashed to a log; demons, the skin on their faces pulling back from their teeth to reveal gums prickly with bone fragment, flecks of eel skin; the devil, paddling his shaggy legs like a pony.

Now and again, a tattered resistance fighter, perhaps, like those the poet saw in Serbia, bloodied, grim, looking off in the distance in a way that suggests a brave soldier seemingly unconcerned that a much larger army stands against him, like one who is posing as reference for an oil painting titled *Martyr to Nationalism.*

At last, the poet stares directly into the depths of the Daugava, imagines a face taking form in the silt:

A boy, but with ears furred and veined like a bear's.

The poet plucks the bear-boy from the river—and writes him into an alternate mythopoetic version of the past. One where he is a foundling, the child of man and bear, chosen specifically by the gods, and lifted from murk of the river where he has been cast, to help unite the Latvians against their occupiers.

In the poet's rendering, the boy is sent by the gods to live with the king of one of the pagan tribes. One day, while they are walking through forest, they are startled by a bear. It charges at the king, but the boy leaps between them and rips the bear's jaw from its head, using only his hands. From this point on, the boy is known as Bear Slayer, and soon after, he sets off to pit himself against witches and demons, and other dark forces, preparing himself for the day he will finally meet the Black Knight, and his army of German crusaders, so bent on breaking and subjugating Bear Slayer and his fellow pagans.

By the time the final, decisive duel arrives, it seems possible that the Bear Slayer, who up to now has only known success after success, might triumph.

But as they clash, the Black Knight manages to slice off both Bear Slayer's ears, having grasped that they are the source of his extraordinary strength.

Stripped of his powers, and reduced to just a man, Bear Slayer fights as hard as he can. He strikes the Black Knight with his sword and splits his armor. The Black Knight in turn breaks Bear Slayer's sword. Weaponless, Bear Slayer launches himself at the Black Knight. They grapple, inching closer and closer to the edge of a cliff. For a moment, it appears as if Bear Slayer will find just enough leverage to tip the Black Knight over the lip. But as the knight tumbles backwards, he grabs hold of Bear Slayer. Together, they plummet into the river from which Bear Slayer first rose. And they vanish.

Unveiled at a time when the former serfs are just beginning to ask, however hesitantly, What is our collective identity?, Who are we?, How shall we think of ourselves?, the poet's portrait of the hero Bear Slayer emerges as a potent metaphor.

It will embed deeply in the emerging national consciousness, to be told and retold, again and again. The character of the Black Knight grows more and more fluid over the years, assuming new incarnations, depending on what the poem's audience needs him to be at any given time.

Still, as heroic national epics go, it's a curious one. Decidedly downbeat. Unresolved. The hero fails—sails off a cliff to his death.

But it's the last lines, in particular, that have always unsettled me, in a way I could never quite name. Something about Harijs's bear story tonight has sent me to the bookshelf in search of the exact text, not because I think Harijs's bear story isn't his own story, but because, sometimes, two very different stories have a way of asking the same question.

In the final lines of the Bear Slayer, we learn, in fact, that the moment that has happened is still happening, that we are all trapped in a kind of eternal time. And this means that the knight and Bear Slayer did not actually disappear to their deaths, but instead remain hidden beneath the water's surface, only to be endlessly resurrected, always returned to precisely the same spot, forced to reenact the same last steps.

They clash. They tear flesh. Briefly, they teeter. Then, they begin their long slow pinwheeling descent toward the water. It never varies, never ends.

In some interpretations, this suggestion of an eternal struggle is said to evoke the promise of transcendence—that the Bear Slayer can never really die, because he was never actually alive to begin with. Other interpretations focus on wording that implies, one day, the Bear Slayer's struggle could in fact end, but that it is up to us, as witnesses, to make it stop, the moment we assume his struggle as our own.

Maybe it's because I'm still thinking about what Harijs said earlier, but tonight, all I can see in the ending is an unbearable weariness—the characters never allowed to relive any other part of their story. Always, they are returned only to their worst last moments, of violence and suffering. Then they must repeat this, over and over and over again.

We are always there, too, watching.

No questions tomorrow, I say, but Ausma is in her room, in Harijs's arms I hope, and I am alone in this dark, with what I know and what I don't know struggling to arrange themselves into some kind of form inside of me.

X

THERE WAS A TIME, in the not-so-very-long ago, when the site of my great-grandfather's death would have served as the very place all new lives together should begin.

Back then, what young couples knew of love came from following the bobbing of torchlight through the bosky dark, away from the sounds of their celebrating families, to the barn. There, a bed would be spread on the floor to hold them on their wedding night, their bodies writing the first faint outlines of a future together in the dust.

My grandparents didn't have a proper Latvian wedding.

They didn't dance for two days straight.

No one wove my grandmother the bride's traditional crown made from the leaves of the bilberry. And at the stroke of midnight, my grandfather did not remove the crown from my grandmother's head with the tip of a sword, then let the crown slide slowly down to the length of the blade to the hilt as everyone watched. My grandmother's mother did not step forward to tie a scarf around my grandmother's bare head, signaling that she was now a married woman. And the next morning, the entire wedding party did not burst into the barn, where the two slept, beating pots and pans, driving the new couple to the nearest spring so they might cup their palms in the icy water, then take turns washing their scent from each other's faces with the tips of their fingers.

My grandparents didn't marry at Lembi, although, unlike Ausma and Harijs, they could have. At that time, Lembi still existed. My great-grandfather was still alive, his fall in the barn, and the beginning of the end of farm, still more than three years off in the distant future.

Instead, my grandmother and grandfather said their vows in a registry office in Riga. They traded what appeared to be plain gold bands, with no other family, save my grandmother's brother, in attendance.

They never spoke much of their wedding, but from what little I had heard, I was left with the image of something somber, intensely private, muted, like the moth-soft scuffling of their voices that I could sometimes hear, in the days when I lived with them, as I lay in my bed in the room just beyond theirs, separated only by an unfinished doorway, whisperings that emerged only in the night, things they didn't want to say or couldn't say when anyone else was around, the unmistakable jagging rhythm of tears.

During those years I lived with my grandparents, I had seen my grandfather grab my grandmother by the hips as she tried to pass when he sat reading the paper at the kitchen table, or when he was perched on the edge of their bed, unlacing his boots with thick, work-bent fingers. He would bury his face in the hollow of my grandmother's back as she bucked and tried to get away from him, but she would be laughing, too, and I sensed that if I had not been there, she would not have been in such a hurry to slip from him. They did not say anything to each other in these moments. What passed between them was silent, physical. My grandfather had never been one to speak effusively, particularly when it came to feelings. He was not free with praise. When he wished to be extremely complimentary, he used the phrase *Not bad*. And if he was feeling especially moved by something: *Pretty good*.

In his later years, however, my grandfather could not talk about my grandmother without his voice catching. *What a beautiful woman—I am the luckiest man*, he would say to anyone and to no one, and then he would paw at the tears that collected in the corner of his one good eye. But such displays of emotion always left him drained and mute, rocking back and forth, until finally he found the strength to reemerge, although by then he would launch into long, rambling stories about economics, the lessons one could learn from Latvia's pork and sugar export policies of the 1930s, the business model of the chicken farm his family used to own in the town of Madona— anything, it seemed, to save himself from being overwhelmed by his feelings again.

Once, at a gathering celebrating my grandparents' anniversary, my grandfather, who had been lost in one of his silences, suddenly turned to me: I know that she loved someone else before me. I know because he was my best friend.

He looked directly at me, his glass eye milky. I already knew her before I met her. My friend told me all about her. As he talked about her, I thought, I hope one day I could have a girlfriend like that. And then I saw her. She had long hair then, two braids down her back. I couldn't stop thinking about her. It hurt, how much I thought of her. So do you know what I did next?

It's why I am here now, grandfather. Wandering this forest about forty kilometers from Ausma's house, having negotiated a ride with a relative this morning, so I can leave her in peace; why I am scanning the bark of every tree I pass, trying not to think of the ticks I am stirring as I stomp through the underbrush. Beneath my feet, a thick carpet of bilberry. I can smell the scent the leaves release as they are crushed under my boots, like a jar of old pennies, the long forgotten drawer of a basement workbench, full of washers, screws, bent nails. I took a knife and I went out behind our school, to the woods, he said, and when I was sure no one could see me, I carved her name into a birch tree.

THIS LAND has always made its own fables, like the one about the children and grandchildren and great-grandchildren of the country's former serfs who came to live in a palace that had once belonged to one of the barons who had ruled them.

The palace was called Cesvaine, and the children slept in its turrets; they sipped cabbage soup in the former grand dining room, where stone bears nearly as tall as they were supported the mantelpiece of a fireplace on their great shaggy shoulders.

The castle was made from stones, placed by architects brought specially from Berlin for the job, the vision of one Adolf Gerhard Boris Emil von Wulf, who should not, under any circumstances, be confused with a von Wolff, a separate baronial dynasty that happened to rule just a few kilometers down the road. This potential for confusion apparently elicited strong feelings in our young master von Wulf. So strong were his feelings, in fact, that when it came time for workers to mount a sculpture atop the pediment denoting the baron's personal wing of his new palace, it was said to be no coincidence that a particularly demonstrative version of his family's lupine mascot was chosen—tail lifted—and aimed in the direction of the rival house.

Von Wulf had designed Cesvaine as a hunting palace, a place where he could mount the skulls of the roe deer and harts flushed from the neighboring forestland. He placed his trophies in careful rows above the castle's tiled hearths, built by German craftsmen. The hounds paced and shed upon hand-laid parquet. Above them, in frescoes painted upon the vaulted ceilings, hawks retired to persimmon-branch perches to tear carp apart with the points of their beaks, while wolves, toothsome and unrelenting, snapped at the spindly legs of a bull moose, one misstep away from becoming carrion. Guests of the baron slept beneath more soothing images, carved reliefs on the walls of each bedroom featuring cherubs so content and fat as to appear kneeless, stomachs lolling happily below the waists of their loincloths.

All this—this land, this title, the means to build these rooms—how much did he allow himself to think about how it had come into his possession, that it was all down to someone else's death, a hunting accident, a blind shot in the woods that felled his father?

In the end, young master von Wulf would have only seven years to enjoy what he had made of that inheritance, this palace with its scenes of flight and pursuit, its cherubs, and cheeky wolf sculpture—as many years as it took him to build it.

He died a few weeks before his forty-seventh birthday, in Vienna, and his body was returned to Latvia to be buried, at his request, on Cesvaine's grounds.

After the baron's death, *little is known about the subsequent events in the castle.* This rather cryptic account is from a history commissioned not long ago by the local council.

I like to picture the interior of the palace during those lost years: empty, still, white sheets draped over the unused furniture, the fug of trapped air, windows long unopened.

And then, the fine layer of dust that covers the floor, the stairs, is stirred, as if by a gentle huff of breath.

Maybe an antler, knocked crooked, slowly rights itself.

Down in the basement, where the servants once dragged blocks of ice cut from the nearby stream to cool the contents of the palace larder, empty jars might suddenly jump and natter upon cobwebbed shelves.

And upon each sheeted bed, in each locked bedroom, a depression appears—always to one side—whichever one he remembers preferring.

I will give him fifteen years to roam like this, undisturbed by the pace of history unfolding outside the castle walls.

And then comes the revolt of 1905.

Even though the country's former serfs, like my great-great-grandfather and his descendants, have lived as free men and women for almost ninety years by this point, most remain landless, unlike my great-great-grandfather and his descendants.

So the peasants venture to Riga, the capital, drawn by stories of electric lights and streetcars, only to find that they still go to bed hungry and frustrated, that the hands of a good milker, the hands that can guide a draft horse at the plow, mean nothing on the assembly lines of the newly opened factories.

One day, some of the frustrated assemble on the banks of the Daugava, which runs through the center of Riga—the river into which Bear Slayer was flung—to try to dredge the depths of their dissatisfaction. High unemployment. Crushing poverty. Imperial rule. No way to change anything. No self-representation. They find that fury rises easily, there on the riverbanks, that they like the way it threatens to surge and crest. They chant and throw stones. The police don't like it, though, and open fire on the crowd. A teenage boy crumples— a member of one of the Jewish labor groups that has been instrumental in organizing the city's workers. Everyone runs. And at last, something breaks open, like the ice that cracks beneath the feet of those who scramble onto the frozen stretch of water, rather than run into the policemen's guns.

The screams beneath the ice travel the Dauguva, echoing deeper and deeper into the Latvian countryside. Seventy-three people shot or drowned. Two hundred injured. As this news from the capital ripples through the remote villages, anger mounts.

For all the promises of freedom and reform since the emancipation of the serfs, nothing has changed. The peasants have no political voice or influence. All the power still rests in the hands of the wealthy German landowners, with the representatives of the tsar.

What happens next is as if everyone suddenly dreams the same waking dream of revenge: across the countryside, the peasants take up torches and rocks, and head to the nearest manor house.

For several days, they burn and they smash, until hundreds of castles and manors across the region have been reduced to ash and bone-char and rubble.

Remarkably, these days of fury do not touch Cesvaine palace.

It sits undisturbed, as the sculpture on the roof swishes his tail in the direction of the other local wolves, who do not slip fury's attention so easily—their den immolated as the live-in servants stand and gawp in their nightclothes.

The ruins have not stopped smoldering when the tsar dispatches troops. Together, with mercenaries hired by the barons, they fly through the occupied lands, executing, burning, flogging. More than two thousand peasants will die, nearly three thousand more shipped to the edges of the known world, to the endless and eternal steppes. And fury slips back under the ice.

A relatively quiet decade passes, in which my grandmother and grandfather are born.

Storks build nests atop Cesvaine's chimneys.

Deer venture closer, with no hounds to drive them back.

From his perch, the palace wolf watches, sword clenched in one paw, always ready.

He has a good view when the marching starts.

All across the countryside, local boys emerge wearing the uniforms of the occupying empire, tsar-approved boiled brown wool that absorbs the kickback of the rifles that they aim at the kaiser's advancing army. But it does not protect them from the winter's bitter cold, so that they take to covering their heads with sackcloth, punching holes only large enough so that their eyes might make out the targets they can lock in their sights. They are completely shrouded, anonymous, an army of ghosts.

Even alive, they are already as good as dead, rabbiting about underground, screaming faceless through the trenches, apparitions emerging and retreating into the chemical fog.

And then Lenin makes his move, and now which uniform shall they wear?

They've just fought on behalf of one occupier, against another potential occupier, as has been done for centuries. But no matter the uniform, the outcome is always the same.

They always fight only for the right to remain ghosts in their own land.

What does it take for a ghost to finally find its voice?

Another country's revolution, a Bolshevik coup, a tsar slaughtered in a basement, a kaiser's losing campaign.

One by one, the distractions mount, until suddenly there's a pause that extends long enough for a man to take the stage of the national theater in Riga and announce, This place is real, this country is real. It exists.

There are still two more chaotic years, years of civil war and uncertainty, before independence is official. But finally, Cesvaine palace, which was once situated at the edge of a frontier known to the rest of the world most recently as Livland, wakes up at the close of World War I to find itself on new ground.

Once, this region answered to many names, organized by its occupiers into duchies, littoral zones, provinces. Now all that has been reclaimed and rechristened as the free and independent republic known as Latvia. And my grandparents are among the first generation to grow up, officially, from the time of their earliest childhood, as Latvians.

Among the republic's citizens, the period leading up to this declaration of independence, of growing national consciousness, is known as the time of awakening—an interesting phrase because it suggests the process of achieving consciousness, but not yet fully inhabiting it.

In the spirit of this state of awakening, someone decides that the perfect setting for adolescence would be a baron's empty castle.

So the new tenants come, dragging trunks up the stairs, palming balustrades with hands blistered from handling harvest scythes.

The first class of Cesvaine arrives in 1919, one year after independence is claimed, farmers' children all of them, transplanted from the fields to this boarding school that will prepare them for a spot in the new national university system, if they so desire.

They are Latvia's future, the inheritors of its awakening, and yet, as soon as they cross the palace threshold, they will occupy a world that operates outside of real time. While their parents and grandparents head out to the fields under a heavy sun, the children gather in the castle's cool ballroom to learn folk dances that mimic the motions of the harvest rituals. As their families bend to drop the seeds, they bend to see their reflections in the polished hardwood floor. As the draft horse clops back and forth to deliver his loads to the granary, they clop from one end of the ballroom to the other. The movements they make are as old as the soil they no longer have to handle, the soil they no longer must dig from under their fingernails.

There are choirs to join, too, in which they sing folk songs, while dressed in the clothes of the ancients, women's waists nipped by belts onto which have been woven the symbols that were used before words existed to call upon the sun and the morning star and the snake who protects us and the god that lives in the grain and the tree through which dawn emerges each morning. But also, just as easily, they slip out of the old costumes and into heels and drop-waisted dresses, smooth their bobbed hair and pose for formal school portraits, which they then carefully paste into photo albums that in just a few years will be abandoned all over again, left in houses from which they are taken, or left in houses that they must flee so that they are not taken.

All that will come later, when time and fury has caught back up with them.

For now, there is only the strange, protected space of the castle.

There is my grandfather, arriving from his family's chicken farm.

He is already starting to turn in on himself, intense and silent, a boy who has learned from an early age that he cannot depend on his parents, who spend most of their time locked behind their respective doors, his father with a bottle, his mother with a bottle, too, but also one of her many dear women friends who come to visit—and then stay overnight. They are an affluent family by the standards of the countryside, but their fortune is emptying as quickly as all those bottles piling behind locked doors.

Years later, the only story he will repeat from this time is how his mother once left a roast unattended on the kitchen counter, and in the time she realized her mistake, the cat had wrestled it to the floor and gnawed it to the bone. He will tell this story in place of all the others he could tell about what he knows of disappearing, of how in a few years his younger sister will stop eating, until there is almost nothing left to bury, the coffin so light it is unbearable to lift.

By the time my grandfather enters the castle he has already shed his attachment to the land, to home. He wants no part of the family farm and its memories. He prefers the certainty of numbers, likes their assurance and solidity. He particularly likes the idea of economics, formulas and models that might render at least some aspects of human behavior predictable. With his round wire glasses and his hair groomed so precisely as to show the path of his comb's every tooth, he looks as if he has just come from a wood-paneled study full of books, where the only sound is the susurration of paper as he flips through his notes, not the feathered, squalling, manure-booted chaos of the poultry farm.

The first friend he makes at Cesvaine is nothing like him—as blond as he is dark, a joker, a tippler, winking and unrestrained. He looks like the land he is from: weathered like the hay that is stacked on racks to dry in the sun, eyes as pale as the petals of flax, a tip to his head like the cricked branch of an oak.

His new friend is always writing letters.

To whom, my grandfather wants to know.

That is when he says her name to my grandfather for the first time.

In two years, she will be old enough to join them at the castle. By then, my grandfather has memorized everything about her. He knows the name of the farm from whence her letters come. He knows the confessions that these letters contain, the secrets she believes she is sharing only with his friend, and is careful to hide from everyone else, especially her father, who is certain she is too young to feel the way she claims she does and has forbidden the relationship, even banned her from speaking the boy's name.

So she writes it.

Maybe this is why one day, not long after she has finally taken her place among Cesvaine's pupils, my grandfather does what he does, why he slips a knife in his pocket and heads out by himself into the forest surrounding the castle, where the baron once stalked his harts, why my grandfather picks the white trunk of a birch, its bark thin like paper.

He cannot tell his only friend that he has fallen in love with his girlfriend. He cannot say her name. So he takes out the knife, presses the point in the bark. And he writes it.

Livija

A few months later, while home on school holiday, his best friend will step on a nail that drives through the flesh of his foot. He will be dead before the holiday is over, under the ground by the time classes in the castle resume. She's too distraught to attend the funeral, too distraught to speak of him when my grandfather tries to approach her in their shared grief.

He leaves the palace soon after, off to Riga for a spot at the university there, and he tries to forget her. He channels all his intensity into his studies, eventually earns his master's degree in economics, and a position at the university as an assistant professor. By day he works for a textile mill, running their books. At night, he teaches. He wears a fedora now and a marten-collared overcoat and carries a briefcase full of student papers. After his evening lectures, he rides the streetcar to the apartment he shares with two others from the university, located next to what looks like a park, dark and wild with ground elder. It is really a mass grave, the site where bodies of Riga's plague victims were once dumped when this was far outside the city limits.

One day, one of my grandfather's flatmates announces his intent to move out, and so the landlady posts a notice in the newspaper. A new tenant is found while my grandfather is off visiting his family, already moved in by the time he returns two weeks later.

It is a shock to both of them when he opens the apartment door to find her standing there.

She has left the countryside to accept a job as a bookkeeper with, as she liked to say because she liked the sound of the phrase, Latvia's leading bacon export factory, and she has been looking everywhere for a place to live that she could both tolerate and afford, crossing off each circled listing one by one, until finally arriving here.

Her room is just down the hall from his, but soon she is no longer using it, instead sharing his single bed.

If he ever wonders whether it is because he is the closest thing she has to what she has lost, he keeps it to himself.

Just as he never talks about the fact that the luck that brought her to him is the result of someone else's misfortune, that the life that grows inside of her is because of someone else's death.

They make an appointment with the registry office.

What they do not yet know, as they take these steps toward what they imagine will be a shared future, is that the future has already been decided, without them:

Because, two years before, right around the time they were finding each other again in the apartment on Peace Street, somewhere in Moscow, men were meeting, too, to pretend they were not speaking of war.

This is what a secret pact looks like:

Men in suits gathered in a paneled room, too many for the small space, their damp handshaking and back-clasping overseen by an unremarkable portrait of Lenin, hunched, severe-looking, as if he is not happy with the messy state of the desk behind which he has been placed for the purposes of the painting. In real life, there is also a desk, buffed to a high polish, fussy with paperweights, ceremonial ink blotter, heavy glass-shaded lamp, magnifying lens. Three rotary telephones. And now, a representative of Hitler's government and a representative of Stalin's government are taking turns placing the nibs of their respective quills to a paper laid upon the desk. And it would appear as if the men are doing nothing more remarkable than simply scratching their signatures on this paper, as Stalin, very much not a portrait, looms over their shoulders. Still, if we were to pick up the magnifying glass that lies in the corner of desk and train it in the direction of Stalin's mustache, we would see, just beneath the screen of it, a grin so unrestrained that the waxed tips of his facial hair appear as if they are levitating, as if electrically charged, trying to conduct Lenin's attention. This is our hint that something more is happening here, something that cannot be seen as it is happening, only in retrospect. And what is happening is this: with their signatures, these men are effectively scratching away the borders of the country once known as Latvia.

Proposed in its place: an undefined block of territory to be known as the *Soviet sphere of interest.*

Publicly, the men will say this meeting was about finalizing an economic trade agreement.

And the agreement is a trade, of sorts.

Russia secretly promises, for the time being, to do nothing so Germany can invade Poland, then Lithuania.

In return, Germany secretly promises, for the time being, to do nothing so Russia can invade Latvia, Finland and Estonia.

When the ink is dry, Germany makes straight for western Poland.

And World War II begins.

It will take some time for the news of this annexation on

paper to actually reach the people of Latvia, who will spend the next three years that follow the secret meeting living as if this no-country is still their home, completely ignorant that its name has been unsaid, that in textbooks and on schoolhouse maps in Russia, children are already learning that Latvia is part of the USSR.

By the time my grandparents finally enter the hushed seclusion of the registry office, the consequences of this secret pact between Stalin and Hitler are becoming painfully clear. In the span of the past twelve months, Latvia has already been invaded twice.

First by Russia, expanding its *sphere of influence*, as agreed upon in the pact.

Then, just a year later, by Germany, when, flush with mounting victories, Hitler decides that perhaps the pact has outlived its tactical usefulness.

And in that small, unremarkable and nearly empty room, which sits roughly in the middle of the two opposing sides, my grandfather places a ring on my grandmother's finger, and she places a ring on his finger.

Together, they attempt their own fragile, muted pact.

Inside his wedding band: an inscription, a wish, a plea.

The same letters he etched in the tree—

Livija

—his incantation against vanishing.

NOT FIFTEEN YEARS AGO, a fire ripped through Cesvaine, as if set by the invisible hands of an angry mob of serfs that had suddenly appeared to complete the unfinished job of 1905. Flames licked largely through the upper floors where students like my grandparents once bunked, but the rest of the castle was spared.

I have come already certain of what I want to find.

Inside, I see the frescoes my grandparents spoke of, the rows of antlers, the bears on either side of the fireplace still supporting the weight of the great mantelpiece.

I run my hand down the wooden banisters smoothed by the years of gripping hands, slip my feet into the grooves carved into the stairs by so many heavy steps.

I spend what feels like hours in the surrounding forest, willing the letters to rise on scarred bark.

But every birch I find is bare, unmarked.

XI

Before the family farm felt war; before it absorbed the difference between the tumbling pitch of a bomb, and that of my great-grandfather's body; before it sheltered my grandmother Livija's youth, then stole Ausma's; before it was lost, then regained, then lost again, as if in imitation of the confused cycles of the country in which it found itself—this is what the eighty acres that would one day be Lembi knew:

For over a billion years, uneventful stillness.

Once the Earth's crust cooled, once the days of rifting and rending ended, this part of the continent chose for itself, at least inwardly, an identity of stability and caution. Geologically speaking, it was not in the land's nature to move or to drift.

Ice came, vast sheets that flowed and stretched and pooled across the land's surface. When enough ice built upon the existing ice, it would walk. Slowly. Grinding everything beneath it flat, dragging with it clots of debris.

When the ice finally began to melt, it left in its wake, upon the scraped and leveled landscape, all that it had gathered, deep tills of sediment, rich hummocky deposits that could be read under the feet like braille.

What passed for hills swelled low, blisterlike beneath the

Earth's skin. The steepest pitched no higher than three hundred of a man's boldest strides.

It must have been a relief, then, to those first settlers who finally stumbled to a halt upon this prone place, those who were said to have walked without direction on leathered feet until at last they reached what felt like the edge of everywhere. There, in the mossy light, amid the sound of grabbling wings and the croaking bogs and the unceasing horizon, they said, We are tired, and this will do, and burrowed like ants under the flat fat blankets of soil.

But the planed relief of their new home, the welcome lack of obstacles also meant that this was a geography that would expose them, that there was nothing to stall the pace of whatever force might be rippling across its surface this very moment.

At least it offered an unobstructed view of their ever-changing futures.

And on this particular June day, in 1940, the land says their future looks like this: the flea-brown tunic of a Russian soldier moving at the edge of the meadow.

This is how the concepts of invasion, occupation, then war announce themselves to Ausma.

It began with the vague hissing of the radio inside the farmhouse at Lembi—*Poland* and *Germany* and *English naval blockades in the Baltic Sea*; letters from her sister in Riga about shop shelves running empty, not a grain of salt in the whole city; the adults discussing rumors that the president is about to send Riga's redundant workers to the countryside to work on the farms, to help the country produce more food; the arguments over the meaning of a government announcement that the country has entered into a *Mutual-Assistance Treaty with Rus-*

sia, and will *open its borders* for the Russians *to establish military bases*, whether this is, in fact, a free choice.

All these words manifesting themselves now in the flea-brown tunic of a Russian soldier, set in silhouette against the June wheat.

It is the summer of Ausma's thirteenth year, and she has been imagining what it will be like to take her turn, finally, at Cesvaine, the boarding school for farmers' children, in the fall.

She has no idea the sighting of the soldier will signal the end of her formal education. Never again will she sit in a classroom, staring at a chalkboard map that tells her she lives in Latvia, while from the back of the room, her husband-to-be secretly studies her studying that map, the cool rivering of her braids, the smart path they cut down the back of her dress, a dress he thinks is beautiful, and which she thinks that she hates, tugging self-consciously at the armpits, another hand-me-down—her clothes are only ever hand-me-downs, darted and unhemmed, rippered and reseamed—left to her by her older sister when she decided to move to the capital.

Where once, her sister, Livija, had come home to Lembi nearly every weekend on the train, dragging back with her grainsacks of potatoes, knobs of cabbage, scoops from her mother's wooden salt box—the countryside has not suffered the way Riga has with the blockades—she has been returning less and less, choosing to stay in the city now that she has fallen in love with someone in Riga. She tells Ausma the story of how they came to be together, meeting first at Cesvaine, then at the apartment on Peace Street, the whole sad, startling story—not her mother, not her father, just Ausma. And Ausma feels, for the first time in her life, like the letters bound in ribbon and addressed to her sister from the boy she loved, which Ausma had found and then rehid among Livija's things.

The next time Livija is back at Lembi, she convinces Ausma that they should ride their bicycles to Emils's family's home, where he is also visiting his parents. It's a long way to go in just a day—nearly forty kilometers—and the sky looks an unpromising color—let us imagine the lilac gray of rotting things. But Ausma likes the feeling of being brought into her sister's confidence too much to care about how tired or how wet she might get. There is something about seeing her sister, typically so poised, almost frantic over the idea of being apart from this man, unable to wait another day to see him back in Riga, when she knows he is this close to her. It's as if she and her sister are coconspirators in something, something as wild and as uncontrollable as the storm that rolls over them while they are still pedaling, pelting them with raindrops fat like splatting plums, hail that pits the skin on their hands and their faces an angry pink.

They reach Emils's house, soaked and chattering, and spend the day in borrowed clothing, pulled from the back of an old wardrobe. This feels nothing like wearing her sister's hand-me-downs, more exciting somehow, like being granted the chance to spend the day in costume, to put on someone else's life. When they ask her how she likes her tea, she asks for only a twirl of honey, like Livija. She sits at the edge of her chair, in front of the fire Emils has made to warm them, and crosses her legs at the ankles, like Livija. She memorizes her sister in this moment, her easy happiness, light as the teacup in Livija's hand, light as Emils's touch on the small of her back as he walks them, with their bicycles, back toward the road, toward home. The sky is turning dark, and so they ride single file, Ausma trailing just behind her sister, watching the last of the sun catch and scatter on the spokes of her tires, letting Livija set the pace. And maybe, later that night, as she rolls over in her bed, back at Lembi, trying to find a comfortable position for her burning, cramping calves, and a wisp of hair catches on her cheek, releasing the dusky smell of dried rain, maybe she thinks this will be her template for what it is to grow up. That all she has to do is follow Livija.

WATCH THE BEES, her brother, Janis, tells her. See where they're flying—today, over to the raspberry cane.

Her brother is twenty-four, and next in line to run the farm, and he has already begun to take over some of its operations.

For as long as anyone can remember, bees have been a part of Lembi, the wooden boxes that serve as their hives spread from orchard to field to forest's edge.

Janis learned to care for the bees from his father, who learned from his father before him, back in the days when they kept the bees in cavities they had carved in trees, and reached by climbing, or in hollow logs. Janis thinks maybe Ausma might have the gift, too.

The bees of Lembi are said to make honey that tastes like time, sweet and sad and ancient, as if it contains all the memories of all the things that had ever grown and died there. Their keepers believe it's because they speak to the bees, soothe them with the touch of their breath, rather than smoke. Where did you go today? they ask. What did you see? When it comes time to open the hives, to remove the racks and cut the capping of wax from the combs that tell them the honey is ready, the bees skim their arms like gossamer sleeves, scarf their skulls as softly as silk handkerchiefs, beard their cheeks like light fuzzings of stubble. They never sting.

Midsummer is the busiest season, the racks so heavy they require four hands to lift, any gaps or cracks around the edges daubed thick with the mixture of bee spit and wax and the resin that rushes like blood from a cut bud or a tree branch, which the bees use to seal their hives, to keep out harmful things. Her brother shows Ausma how to scrape at the red braids of it with the edge of a knife, to save it in jars, as a salve for cuts or burns, as a balm for toothaches, for mouths that erupt in sores. He knows by the subtle variation of yellows and browns in the pollen on their legs which flowers they have visited, heather or clover or buckwheat, although she can't see it yet.

As he works, her brother sings to the bees: *One day, I will brew beer, and I will keep you in my pocket while I do it, so that anyone who drinks from my bottles will feel their heads trilling like your wings!*

The sound of the bees is calming, like sleeping while you're still awake. She loves the way they seem to return to the same hives, like the cows entering the barn each night, always tramping without any prompting into their own stalls. And when you shake into your open palm the cakes of pollen that the bees tamp down like secrets in the bottom of their cells, then press them against your lips, it's almost possible to imagine you are tasting their memories, a flavor that is at once lush and chalky and acrid, like touching your tongue to humus or bone.

And then, one day, Ausma is stung.

The way her skin puckers and blooms, they know this will put an end to her apprenticeship.

She watches from a distance now.

Inside the house, her mother Alma sleeps. No one can say what's wrong with her, what's left her so weak, pinned to the bed, like a bee with wet wings.

LATER, IT WILL BE EASY to see this as the summer when all the loss that is to come reveals itself to her at once, using the cover of visible things, like when they would pour spoonfuls of molten lead into a pail of water on the first night of the new year, searching the twists and folds for a likeness in the living world, a shape to which they could attach a narrative that would foretell the future.

But when she first spots the Russian soldier moving through the fields, she's not thinking of signs or portents. She's not thinking about much of anything, except for cows, bees, bicycles, Cesvaine, her sister's new love.

It's the first foreign soldier she has seen, outside of books. And he looks so small. A bee far from the hive.

Then she sees the long solemn columns, clodding the roads. Next, the tanks slowly, deliberately snailing their way toward Riga. They chew runnels in the roads that make the horses balk for weeks.

Later, inside the farmhouse, when they turn on the radio, it crackles with news that is not so much news, as aphorism.

I am remaining in my place, you remain in yours, says Latvia's president, a former dairy farmer, who in his youth, was among those seized after the unrest of 1905, briefly imprisoned, before fleeing to America to avoid further punishment, to the state of Nebraska, where they also love cows. He spent several years there, before deciding to return to Latvia just in time to assist in the country's fight for her independence, and became a significant force in the emerging government, a darling of the agricultural party.

Then, he took control in a bloodless coup, saying the good of the country demanded a firm hand, clear guidance, as if a country were one of his milk cows, not producing as she should. People seem not to know whether to admire him or detest him for his totalitarian ways, a benevolent dictator, if such a combination is even possible, who has achieved the illusion of unshakable national unity—*Latvia's sun shines equally over everyone!*—by clamping down on any dissenting voices, outlawing all political parties, scrapping parliament, muzzling the press. Small things, some people argue, when you consider what he has done for Latvia's economy, how well they are doing, relatively speaking, for such a small nation, and how quickly he has boosted the profile of its farmers, sold the rest of the world on the singular quality of her butter and bacon.

I am remaining in my place, he says, as Russian tanks ring Riga. *You remain in yours.*

A few weeks later, he is deported.

New government, the radio stutters.

Then: *Welcome to the Soviet Republic!*

THAT PUTS AN END to summer, and now fall is approaching, but on the subject of Cesvaine, Ausma's parents are silent. Later, she will hear a rumor that the Soviets claimed the castle after their arrival, requisitioned it for something other than classes, accommodations for officers, perhaps, important people in the Party. She has no idea if that's true. All she knows is that the start of the school year has come and gone, and someone is sleeping in the castle of her sister's stories, and it's not her.

Ghosting about the farm, she catches fragments of the adults' conversations, rough like the trimmings of the horse's hooves that her father leaves scattered on the floor of the barn for the dogs to tooth. Collectivization, she hears her father's friends saying, and they spit the words like it's something turning in the bottom of an unwashed glass. Never, they say and shake their wooly heads, making the beer they grip with their chapped hands swirl and tremble.

Her father pulls down a new bottle.

Then another.

Disappeared, she hears another time. The whole family. No one knows where.

Which is not entirely true.

Someone somewhere knows.

Across the country, inside unmarked buildings, files are accumulating.

And inside these files: names.

Unreliables. Enemies of the people. Individuals the newly installed secret police suspect could prove *disruptive* in this time of transition and unification.

The consequence of being one whose name appears in such a file is revealed slowly at first, one person at a time, so that it's easy to convince yourself what's happening can't really be happening, easy to invent stories that somehow make more sense than what must be the truth.

The schoolteacher who one day doesn't show up for work. Bent over double with a stomach gone sour? Or the minister who doesn't come to unlock the church door on Sunday. Laid up with the gout? The newspaper editor who speaks Esperanto— on one of his binges, most likely, just give him a week and he'll resurface, split-lipped, hickeyed, memory scoured, repentant.

But as the unmarked buildings begin to fill with files, great drifting mounds of files, and one hundred people begin to disappear each month, then two hundred people, then three hundred, these absences, and the unspoken implication behind each of these absences, are becoming harder to ignore.

Soon, the loved ones of the missing no longer bother to report them missing. They understand now that no one in the unmarked buildings will ever tell them whether there is a file. Or whether the file says *Gulag*. Or whether it says, *Execute by firing squad*.

Inside the unmarked buildings that are rapidly filling with secret files that no one will admit the existence of, the gatherers of these individual names would not mind some additional flexibility in assigning fates. Something between a death sentence and a prison sentence. Something like a bureaucratic order that could apply, immediately, to thousands.

For this, they begin to turn to the idea of forcible resettlement. *Special exile.*

To designate someone a special exile is to be freed from the bother of ever staging a trial. No need to accuse someone of a specific crime, only to imply that they fit one of twenty or so preapproved categories that are fast tracks to banishment, general enough that they could apply to almost anyone. A government-ordered change of address that catches thousands unaware, and comes without warning.

Just a knock. Usually in the early hours of morning. So that you will be half-asleep, cotton-headed, slow to grasp what is happening, what it means when *the senior member of the operative group* tells you to gather everyone in your family into one room, while *taking all necessary precautionary measures against any possible excesses,* so that you can be *notified that upon the decision of the Government you are being deported to other regions of the Union.*

Do they give you time to pack? Do they tell you the items you are officially permitted to bring?

One suit.

Or are you dreaming that?

Do the neighbors come out to see what is happening? Are they *called upon to disperse to their homes?* Is not a word allowed to pass between you and *any passersby?*

Would you say what is happening to you is *firm and decisive . . . without the slightest pomposity, noise and panic?*

And once you are loaded into your designated railcar—*an estimated 25 persons per car should be observed*—can you hear the door lock?

These are the protocols as prescribed by the Third Deputy People's Commissar of State Security of the USSR, an exhaustive list of how-tos for those needing guidance on such subjects as the Manner of Executing Deportation, the Manner of Separating the Deportee from His Family, the Manner of Conveying the Deportees and the Manner of Embarking.

The commissar is a man named Ivan Serov, stocky, with blue-gray eyes and a knack for engineering mass exile. Calm, deliberate, methodical, he excels at anticipating each step, right down to the moment the bolt should be thrown across the door.

He is honing his skills, perfecting his method, squinting

his blue-gray eyes off into the Soviet future, when he will run the KGB.

Already, his résumé includes the recent exile of a million and a half Poles. Tens of thousands of Crimeans. Ukrainians. Gone. Later, it will be Hungarians, teenagers mostly, thought likely to join the resistance, hustled off beneath the streets and loaded into train cars, the doors locked tight.

In Latvia, his secret police identify more than fifteen thousand candidates for a single operation of mass exile. Several thousand from Lithuania and Estonia, too. After months of planning, they pick a day: June 14, 1941.

Mostly, for this round—because the planning has already begun for another round—it's intellectuals, the political elite, soldiers, businessmen, even Boy Scouts who are targeted—and never just an individual, but their entire families. Jews, Russians and Poles who also call the country home. And while the whole family is taken together, they will not stay together. The men will be sent to labor camps, the women and children to special settlements.

At least for those sent to the Gulags, there is some kind of internal infrastructure, a crude logic at work: places to sleep, however rough, regular meals, however meager. When the special exiles are finally coaxed blinking from the boxcars that dragged them through the Urals, across the overwhelming steppes, they're simply left in the middle of nowhere, instructed to fend for themselves. There are no daily breadlines, no fences or guard towers. The land is so unforgiving, it forms its own prison. Stripped of everything, carrying only what they had time to pack, the special exiles must start over again. They must secure their own shelter. They must feed and clothe themselves.

But even as they're left to engineer their own survival, they are also expected to help the architects of their exile. They are all workers now for the Soviet State.

And so, for the good of the state, they will drag saws through Russian pine, clear meadows in the summer with scythes, harvest milk from the spindly Siberian cows of the sad collective dairies, descend newt-eyed into mines.

A pen scratched them out of existence, now it will record their every move: who reports to work, how much they saw and stack. Exhaustion from starvation does not excuse anyone from their work.

If one can be said to be lucky in such situations, the lucky ones will be delivered to areas where, maybe, there's already a small, weathered community of existing exiles. Descendants of tsarist-era dissidents, or more recent arrivals, those shipped to the territories in the east within the last ten years—when the Soviet Union began its early experiments in the collectivization of all farmland, and officials realized the process would go much more smoothly if they simply banished a farm's former owners rather than risk resistance. In these settlements, where about half of the newly arrived will die in the first year, from starvation or exposure, the presence of anyone who understands what it will take to endure means you might make it. Someone who is willing to share their crude tools, to offer a place on the floor of their dugouts, or at least to offer to barter bare necessities for whatever strange things the newcomers packed—a suit?—when they did not know what to pack.

Even better: maybe the settlement will have managed to establish a rough working collective, with a bare share of food in exchange for one's labor, a scratching of rations in the form of mealy grain, perhaps, whether offered, or pocketed.

As far as the Soviet officials are concerned, there is no downside to this arrangement: every day that the exiles can survive is another day of unanticipated labor in a region rich in resources that would otherwise go unclaimed.

And if the exiles die—and more than half of these exiles will—then, that's another problem taken care of, too.

IN THOSE EARLY DAYS, the story of the missing is a story they tell one another without saying a thing, the anxious transmissions of a hive mind, the entire village babbling silently to itself, as if suddenly, everyone is the old woman who can no longer remember her name, who bickers with her shadow, pitches pebbles at the sun, sucks the filth from her hands as if it's really sweets.

A list of the things they thought they saw that they did not know whether they should admit to anyone else:

The farmer's wife and her children, led from their own house, their fronts still dusted from making the morning's bread. The neighbor's cat that never crossed the threshold of the barn, that directed its wormy rump at anyone who tried to make eye contact, emerging from your peonies, jittery, dropping fleas, pleading for food. The little man well placed in the local Party, who is now sitting on a pile of pillows, driving the buggy you could swear belonged to the blacksmith.

They react like a village of strangers. Each thinking no farther than the borders of his own life. And in this way, dread becomes something both secret and shared.

It trails Ausma for an anxious week, plodding just behind her, a phantom presence that makes her uneasy in a way that can't be put into words.

Like the moment a fish's belly slips through the knife's slit? No.

Like the egg, when rapped against a bowl, that disgorges bits of unformed chick, pale dimpled skin, a streaking of beak, the suggestion of an eye?

That's not right, either.

Best to stop there, to quit trying.

Some things don't need to be put into words that anyone else can understand.

This is hers and hers alone, the dread of a thirteen-year-old girl.

And it follows its own logic:

Because dread is a secret thing, and the future is a secret thing, now the future becomes something to dread.

Wake to the sound of the stars. Stumble out to the cows. Place your pail so that you can lean into their warm flanks while you work, let them steam your skin when they reach back with their noses to nudge you, testing whether you are just a fly. Then close your eyes and half-sleep while you tug the milk from them. Know how much you have already done by the way the pail sings. Try not to think about how much you don't know, such as whether today could be the day that your mother is imagining when she cries from the nest that is her bed and says she wishes your sister would come home, so that whatever is going to happen, we can at least be together when it happens, and your father says, or are you dreaming, shh, let her have her life, while she can.

———

BOMBS TELL YOU they are coming by the sound of your brother's voice, something held together with sinew and bone, like a hand in your back, driving you underground, into the cold cellar.

BELOW THE LEVEL where anything can grow, they wait, like bolted seeds.

Just a week has passed since the last trains pulled away from Latvia, carrying all those thousands of unspoken names east. And now, this is when the German troops choose to launch a surprise attack against the Russians, and claim Latvia for their own.

They send their planes to Riga first, dropping bomb after bomb, until vast sections of the city are little more than pumiced swales, steaming mounds of slag, the spaces previously occupied by buildings suggested only through negative space; when all that is left is what surrounds what is not there.

That which still manages to stand looks spun, not built.

Seen from above, it's almost possible to pretend Riga is no longer a city, but a vast flattened field where, in the cool of the early morning, before a foot or a hoof has touched the grass, hundreds of spiderwebs might suddenly appear visible to the naked eye, each spare strand latticed with dew.

Down in the cold cellar in Gulbene, in the rooted dark, they listen to the zippering shriek of the planes, and hope that Livija is also somewhere safe, wherever she might be in Riga. The earth relays the only news they receive from the surface, dribblings of dirt and earthworm casings in patterns that communicate the concussive forces of the various forms of ordnance, antiaircraft rounds launched from the ground, bombs dropped from the skies, aerial skirmishes, hit or miss, miss or hit, near, far, near, near, far.

When, finally, they climb to the surface, they see scorched sections of road, smoldering bits of fuselage, blistered fields. But Lembi still stands. Somewhere, in the distance, a horse is screaming, whether in distress or fear, it is impossible to tell.

Next come the Russian ground troops, trailing German tank fire, the sparking cut of machine guns, their uniforms smoke-soaked, their faces furred and singed from the carbon particles released by the torches they've touched to the roofs of the farmhouses that appear on their path of retreat. But first, they lift all possible supplies, raid the larders, liberate equipment and horses. Then they flint the matches. Their goal in retreat is to leave the Germans nothing, by taking everything from the peasants.

At Lembi, they track the path of the German advance and the Russian retreat by the graying of the sky. The candling incandescence of the signal flares replace the regular rhythm of sunrise and sunset. They know they lie in the path of the fighting. They do not want to leave Lembi, but they also don't want to be caught in the crossfire. So they round up the animals, eyes rolling, trailing nervous snot. They pack the wagon as if they are never coming back, and head for a clearing, deep in the forest, where they will hide along with some of their neighbors.

Days pass. No one sleeps. That includes the animals, bleating and wheeling, tangling their leads, pissing on themselves, mouths foamy with grass and worry.

Ausma feels their lathering fear. She works her jaw, tries to rid herself of the clenching pain that she's grown to suspect is a bad tooth. She's rubbed her gums with the salve they make from what they find in the bees' hives, held compresses to her swelling cheek, but the pain won't break. She sweats through her clothes, then shivers under blankets. When she opens her eyes she is not sure if it is fever that makes her see a figure emerging from the forest.

It is a German soldier, and she can't understand much of what he says. She has been out of school for so long now that she is struggling to recall her language lessons—and soon, the Germans will requisition the school where Ausma might have gone back, if life had ever returned to normal, which it will not, the new occupying forces claiming it now for the convalescence of wounded soldiers, so that the few German words Ausma still possesses in this moment will be the extent of all she will ever learn of the language, at least formally.

The soldier is speaking directly to her, pointing to the hand she holds to her cheek. She thinks he is asking her what's wrong, that maybe he is trying to establish whether she has been wounded. Finally, she blurts out what she thinks is the word for *pain*. She opens her mouth, points to her tooth. Pain, she repeats.

The German nods, dips his hand into a supply bag. In his palm, a pill, no bigger than a seed. He offers it to Ausma, motions for her to place it in on her tongue.

She swallows it without water. And almost immediately, the pain is gone. Someone translates: the German soldier is telling everyone that they can go back to their farms now—the fighting is over. The Russians are defeated, and the country has been *liberated*.

She looks at this soldier who has just shown her this kindness, however small. Later, she will hesitate remembering the moment, a grave misreading of right and wrong that she otherwise would not have regarded herself capable of, but this is what she thinks, in that moment, in the dark of the woods, the pain momentarily leaving her: maybe life will be better now with the Germans.

XII

THE GRANDFATHER of my memories strips down to his white undershirt, the elastic braces on his pants still hitched up over his bare shoulders. I watch—maybe four years old—as he stands before the old bathroom mirror, clouded as a cataract, holding his left eye in one hand. Careful not to drop the eye in the basin or on the floor where the glass could chip, he runs it under the tap, rinsing it with a gentle stream of warm water. When he is finished, he uses his free hand to pry the skin around his left eye wide, and for an instant, the cavity carved more than thirty years ago by the Russian soldier's bullet is visible. Then, with a muffled pop, he wedges the eye back into its socket.

HE IS ALWAYS trying not to think about the last image that he saw with both eyes. If only it had been his wife, and the pale down on her postchildbirth belly, still stretched to fit the shape of their first son, conceived four months before he received his orders to the front. Or the view from their apartment, where he used to lie with her in the days before the war, the two of them on the narrow bed, knowing what was just beyond the window, the tramline, and the cemetery just beyond that, the graves overgrown and unmarked, dating back to the days of the plague, when bodies could not be buried within five miles of Riga's old center for fear of contagion. Or even a formula, drawn on the chalkboard, back when he still taught economics—AFC + AVC, or maybe, MV = PT—white dusting the hairs of his knuckles on his writing hand, round glasses sliding down his nose.

THE BULLET pierces the metal bridge of his glasses first. The eye is gone before he even registers the loss. Initially, there is no pain, only the sound of his boots on packed earth as he staggers back through the trenches, over bodies, toward someone who might help.

FOR THE PAST FEW DAYS, they have been counting rounds, watching their munitions slowly disappear shot by shot, wondering, bellies to the ground, when the forest will stop firing at them. They have laid a clutch of mines at the edge of the trees and strung a fence of barbed wire that spasms with each blast. But they know that none of this will be enough to hold back the gathering Russian troops, who outnumber them ten to one.

What matters now is not whether they can defend this line, but for how long. They are all that is left to keep the Russian army from advancing on the capital, eighty kilometers away.

The calculus at work is desperate, simple: each additional moment they can absorb the Russian onslaught gives someone in Riga the chance to flee, and all the soldiers seem to have someone in Riga, including him. What is left then but to load his remaining rounds, and hope that this is what she is doing, running, that she does not stop, there is no time for hesitation. There is only time for her to sweep up their two children and leave. Leave it all: the window and the narrow bed. Leave everything, including him.

They run out of ammunition on the second day of fighting. The blood has churned the dirt of the trenches to mud in places. He still has a grenade, his pistol. The silence in the forest, the sound of his own breath, should tell my grandfather that the Russians are on the move, slipping under the barbed wire, creeping toward the ten-kilometer-long trench that has sheltered the Latvian troops. Soon, they are skittering over the lip like spiders.

For the next two days, they fight with their hands, with whatever is at hand, the narrow passageways of the trenches breached, overrun. There is always a press of the enemy's brown uniforms, emerging ahead of you, or behind you, guns drawn. The moment will come when your back is turned, and they are nearly upon you. And something, a twitch, a mote, a flicker of red from a uniform collar, snags on my grandfather's consciousness. And the pin is out before he can even think. And now the grenade is wheeling from his hand toward the Russian soldiers, their turned backs, feet digging into dirt for purchase, as they try to flee. And now he is running through the smoke, and the black and the ash of what remains, running in the direction of their retreat, pushing deeper and deeper into the trench after them.

The man with the gun is just around the corner. They surprise each other. It is an officer, a Russian captain, identifiable by the leather belt cinched at his waist. And clipped to that, the empty holster from which his pistol has already been withdrawn, hammer back.

Together, they fire. This will be the last thing my grandfather sees with both eyes. As he squeezes the trigger of his pistol, he turns his face away, toward the packed earth walls that surround him.

> *Oh, sparrow, when will you take a wife?*
> *In autumn, fall time, time of the barley.*
> *All the birds were invited to the wedding,*
> *Only owl was not invited.*
> *Owl went uninvited,*
> *And sat at the end of the table.*
> *Sparrow asked the owl to dance;*
> *Owl trampled sparrow's foot,*
> *Sparrow pecked out owl's eye.*

HE WAS CONSCRIPTED, that was all he would say about his time in the war.

Conscripted into the Latvian Legion.

And that is all true, but the longer I remain in Latvia, the more clearly I can see that there are some truths that can become more damaging than any lie. Truths built from omission.

When my grandfather fought that day in the battle in which he lost his eye, it is true that he fought as a conscript of the Latvian Legion. But it is also true that technically, even as someone who was drafted into the legion, and not a volunteer, he fought for Germany. He wore a German uniform. It is also true that within the structure of the Nazi military, the legion was classified as a formation within the Waffen S.S., even though, as members of one of the several ethnic legions established in countries occupied by Germany during the war, they were not considered by the Nazis to be *genuine* S.S., more like cannon fodder for the front lines.

These are the things I know now. Things I did not know then.

But because my grandfather never spoke of the war and his part in it, I had always sensed, even as a child, that it must have been a source of tremendous guilt and shame, a suffering so awful that he did not want to think about it. And yet, as he silently rocked and shook and cried in his chair in front of the TV, the sound blaring, an old man, liver-spotted, fragile-boned, it was clear he could not block the memories of what he had seen when he still possessed two good eyes.

In goes the eye.

And it's July 1, 1941.

The day the one army retreats from Latvia, taking with it its hammers and sickles, and Serov's NKVD officers and their thousands upon thousands of secrets, some of which will soon be unearthed from mass graves beneath the prison where everyone suspected the disappeared were taken and questioned. Other secrets—specifically the more than fifteen thousand now just two weeks into their journeys east, still locked in their train cars, but already dying—will remain, a bewildering and unresolved haunting of horror, confusion and rage.

And another army enters, readying swastikas and yellow stars.

Briefly, the country's national anthem warbles over the radio. And then, as the German tanks roll into Riga's center, the radio begins broadcasting a new call to loyalty: those interested in volunteering for a special branch of the *auxiliary police* to rid Latvia of *traitors*, including Communists and Jews, should report at once to the headquarters being established in Krisjana Valdemara Street, quarters *requisitioned* from a local Jewish banker.

Even today, some Latvians say that it wasn't until after the German troops arrived that the savagery began, that it was their presence which began to turn something in people, but that version of events would mean ignoring the women who, on July 1, 1941, have just appeared on Riga's main boulevard dressed in folk costumes, braids bouncing, as they offer bites of bread and shots of vodka and their upturned mouths to the incoming S.S. officers. It would mean ignoring the men, speaking Latvian to one another, who have gathered down in the basement of the banker's former home on Krisjana Valdemara Street, securing plastic sheeting to the walls, something to catch the anticipated sprays of blood. It would mean ignoring the line of volunteers that has already formed outside the building with its plastic-sheeted basement, hundreds by one estimate, many wearing the colors of the fraternities from the University of Latvia, where my grandfather teaches. It would mean turning our eyes away from the Jewish man who is being beaten by men in suits, as if they have just stepped away from their desks, at the feet of a statue of the writer Rudolfs Blaumanis—the author of the novel *In the Lap of Happiness*—in broad daylight, in one of the city's busiest parks.

Within twenty-four hours, Riga's major newspapers publish the following notices: Jews must surrender all property;

they may no longer ride on public transportation or use sidewalks; they may not own radios; they may no longer stand in any lines and must only shop in places where there are no lines.

That night, men wearing armbands in the colors of the Latvian flag roam the city, going door to door, looking for all Jewish residents. Many landlords are happy to direct them to the proper apartments. Once the doors open, the beatings begin, then lootings, and finally, *arrests.* The prisoners are marched in columns down the streets of Riga to the headquarters on Valdemara Street, where they are then led to the basement, but not before they are stripped of all valuables, rings and watches, which their jailers take a moment to enter into a ledger, then slip onto their own fingers and wrists.

Within forty-eight hours, men are digging pits in the forests just outside Riga, making them deep enough to hold thousands of dead.

With seventy-two hours, smoke chokes the city as its synagogues burn. Trapped congregants pound on doors that have been locked from the outside by young men who stand guard to make sure no one escapes. Some people try to exit through the windows, but the men surround anyone who makes it to the street. They bludgeon the escapees with the butt ends of guns. Meanwhile, out in the forests, in the dark, the first wave of prisoners is pushed toward the edge of the pits. A firing squad of ten stands on the other side. After they unload all their bullets, a man with a machine gun roams the edge of the pit, looking for any survivors, then gives the signal for the diggers to cover it all back up. But the killers are all drunk, rushing, and sometimes they refill the hole before everyone is dead. Some see the soil moving, rippling, but they don't do anything, except ask for more vodka.

Out in the countryside, the reaction has been just as fierce and swift. In Gulbene, my grandmother's region of Latvia, census takers, in the years just before the war, recorded the number of Jewish residents to be 84. But within days of the German troops' arrival, every single one of them has vanished, rounded up by soldiers, directed by the local police, who know where everyone lives. Then they are taken to the local train station, where they are held in outbuildings, until the day the blue buses arrive.

The blue buses come from Riga, requisitioned from the city's fleet, filled with the volunteers who have perfected their methods in the forest killings and synagogue burnings and basement tortures. They meet the train carrying Gulbene's Jews about twenty kilometers from the village, then lead the men and women and children to a former army shooting range, where they are slaughtered four at a time, their bodies dumped in a single mass grave.

When the Nazis first marched into Latvia, there were an estimated 70,000 Jews living in the country.

Just three months later, a status report is sent to commanders in Germany. On a map of Latvia, there is a coffin. Above it is written the number 35,238.

It is October 1941.

That month, my grandparents conceive their first child.

A month later, they marry.

By then, nearly every remaining Jew in Latvia will have been murdered.

I HAVE NOT found evidence that my grandfather was a participant in the atrocities that took place in Riga, or the Latvian countryside, or that he condoned them. But there is his silence. It is impossible to imagine that he did not witness what was happening throughout the city, that anyone who lived in Riga at that time could not have seen the smoke and smelled the fires; the neighboring apartments, suddenly empty; the columns of men and women and children being marched down Freedom Street at gunpoint; the barbed wire cordoning off a twelve-square-block section of the city, with a sign outside, in both German and Latvian that reads *Persons who climb the fence or attempt to communicate with ghetto inhabitants through the fence will be shot on sight.* The trains arriving every day, delivering Jews from other countries to the ghetto.

And yet, the outlines of his life in 1941 suggest that my grandfather is trying to live as if none of this is happening, as if he is trying to make his presence smaller and smaller, so that no one will notice him pretending not to notice.

Each morning, he rises and waits for the tram. He goes to his job at the textile factory, and balances the books. At night, he teaches. He stands at the chalkboard. He writes. He erases. He takes the streetcar home.

He slides under the blankets next to my grandmother, who moves his hand to meet their baby's kick.

In July 1942, nearly one year to the day the Nazis arrived in Riga, she tells him it is time.

THE BABY has dark hair, thick and unruly, like her father's.

They name her Maruta.

He buys a camera, holds it up to his eye, fixing her in the viewfinder: such a tiny thing tucked in the crook of her mother's arm, sucking the folds of fabric that wrap her.

But while that camera is pressed against his eye: the German high command is fretting over its losses. They are hemorrhaging soldiers, losing ground to the Russians. They managed to recruit several hundred Latvian volunteers without any trouble. Then they formed a separate unit they called the Latvian Legion, hoping to appeal to Latvian nationalism by giving them their own division, commanded by their own officers. But that's still given them nowhere near enough bodies.

As talk begins of a mandatory induction, my grandparents bundle baby Maruta, just ten months old, and take a train from the city to spend a few days at Lembi, as if a country retreat might let them pretend that there is a parallel universe from the one unfolding in Riga, a world where it was still possible to believe that people could do simple, unthinking things like gather lettuce while the baby gums dirt, or put a stick in her hand and let her wave it at the unamused pigs. Where her uncle will hoist her onto the back of a bored plow horse flicking its tail at her kicks as if they were little more than the touch of settling flies. And where her aunt Ausma, just fourteen, can hold her and sing to her and let her lick sweet batter from her fingers while Livija sleeps.

Maybe it is moments like this that convince my grandfather over the next six months, following that visit to Lembi, that he can go on pretending indefinitely, blocking out the truth of what is happening all around him, and his place in it, especially when his birthday falls just outside the first induction order, issued at the end of 1943.

That month my grandfather Emils and my grandmother Livija conceive their second child, my father.

———

No one reads the newspapers in Riga anymore for news. In fact most people have forgotten what news looks like, what it was to read about the yearly accumulation of rainfall, or the health of the national rye crop, or a review of a performance of Verdi's *Aïda* at the Opera House, or a report on the annual gathering of regional folklorists. Instead, the papers carry statements, proclamations, polemics, bulleted items now preceded by the word *WARNING*. In late March 1944, my grandfather's conscription order arrives. His brother-in-law, my grandmother's brother, Janis, has already received his call-up. Not long after my grandfather's order arrives, the following appears in one of the city's newspapers, under the words *FINAL WARNING*:

> Unconscious citizens who refrain from fulfilling their responsibility to their nation at this decisive moment and have not heeded the instructions will not be able to live unaffected. Sooner or later they will receive the punishment they deserve.

There are men who resist, who take to the forests, who run. But most, like my grandfather, choose to accept their call-up. Some of the men say it does not matter what uniform they wear, they are not fighting for the Germans, they are fighting to protect Latvia, fighting against the Soviets—and when they defeat them, they will turn against the Germans. Still, when they pull the army-issue tunics over their heads, the elbows hollowed to fit the shape of their previous owners, how can they deny the S.S. bolts at the collars?

At his induction, my grandfather and his fellow conscripts repeat the following: *I swear by God this holy oath that in the struggle against Bolshevism I will give the Commander in Chief of the German Armed Forces, Adolf Hitler, absolute obedience and as a brave soldier I will always be ready to lay down my life for this oath.*

At home, on his last leave, he raises the camera once more:

Maruta, her hair dark as a rook's wing, plump-legged like a pony, given, alternately, to gumming a toy dog or closing her eyes against the winter-thinned sunlight. These are the last images of the family, together in Latvia, and even though my father is not yet present, he is already there with them, cells dividing, multiplying, an unseen partner in the moments unfolding.

My grandfather is largely absent from the record of these last days, as if he has already started to hold himself apart, choosing instead to control their framing, lingering on images of mother and child, using the several seconds' stillness required to take a photograph with his old camera as an excuse to memorize their features: Maruta's tiny ears, whorled and vulnerable, like snails unshelled; her first milk teeth, fluttering at the edge of lips callused from breast-feeding; the lines that appear around the edges of his wife's eyes when she smiles, soft like the creases traced in the dirt after a sudden rain; the base of her neck, the way it hollows when she looks down to admire the girl in her lap.

Only a few times, he crosses over to join that life inside the frame: his hands, large and rigid as garden spades, gloved in leather, military issue, Maruta's twig-fingers lost in his grip as he helps her take her first toeing steps.

He is assigned to combat on the eastern front, where Latvia borders Russia. They go without training, with hand-me-down guns and severe shortages of supplies. According to a report from the colonel who headed my grandfather's division:

> Of the 536 horses we were promised, we received only 85, 5 of which were lame. Of the estimated 15 light vehicles there were only 2; of the estimated 18 heavy vehicles, only 2. . . . The soldiers received nothing to drink out of or any eating utensils.

This is how my grandfather will spend the next six months, with dwindling ammunition, under heavy attack, each day bringing him closer to the battle that will claim his eye. Shelled from one side, pinned by tank fire from the other. Guerrilla snipers hidden in the forest canopy, picking off thirty men in a single sustained barrage. One day, while under fire, their commander sends them across a river, storm-swollen, raging. One soldier drowns. The rafts carrying the heavy weapons, and what is left of their ammunition, sink like stones.

The soldiers know before anyone has to tell them: this is a retreat.

What is left of my grandfather's division crosses back into Latvia at the end of July, and suddenly my grandfather is marching through the countryside where he was raised, past farms and barns and horses too old to be afraid of the bombs; past the turnoff for Cesvaine, where he and my grandmother first met; past the former army shooting range, and the unmarked mass grave that holds the bodies of every Jew who once called this area home, too.

He is marching past houses emptied of all life, the inhabitants off to forests to try to hide from the mortar bursts.

One of my grandfather's fellow soldiers, whose job it is to collect the wounded and dying, checks each abandoned house for pillows, which he confiscates so that after he has given each man a gulp of cognac, the only analgesic left, he has something soft to place under their heads.

Abandoned farm animals roam the roads: a pregnant sow, tits dragging on the ground. One of the soldiers shoots it, then guts it, leaving the piglets and viscera in a mound.

By the time my grandfather reaches the site of the battle that will take his eye, his son will have been born. Maybe my grandfather knows. Maybe this is why he and the others do what they do, digging in, facing the onslaught, knowing that their ammunition will not last, that this is likely their end.

There are some Latvian historians who say that the battle in which my grandfather was wounded was critical in giving tens of thousands of refugees like my grandmother time to flee the final violent tremors of the war as it played out in Latvia. A sacrifice, they call it. But the word for *sacrifice* in Latvian can also mean victim, casualty. There are other historians who say that it can never matter why a person fought with the Germans, whether or not their service was mandatory, whether or not they say they only ever served on the Russian front, whether or not they insist that their actions were never meant to help the Reich, but simply, to defend the idea of their former nation, their own families against Bolshevism. Because every day that you helped delay the advance of anyone who was on the side of the Allies, was another day you helped delay the end of the war. And each day you delayed the end of the war was another day you gave the Nazis time to commit additional war crimes.

All those years, as I watched my grandfather convulse and

cry in silent agony, I never once considered that maybe he hurt so badly not because of the wounds he received that day, but because he had not died.

Instead, he woke up in a field hospital, stripped of his uniform, his head bandaged, the chart at his feet noting the extent of the damage that is caused by a single bullet as it enters the eye socket, passes through the impossibly small pocket of space between brain and skull and exits just behind the ear.

XIII

DEEP IN THE BARN, a cow pushes, water breaks upon straw. The first hoof emerges. Then another. One calf drops. Then another. Twins. Their birth-slick bodies steaming in the gloom of the barn. Their mother licks them clean of blood and shit and afterbirth with her bark-rough tongue. Her teats are emptied, and the barn cats shoot from their dens in the hay to fight over the splashes. Some of her milk is set aside for the babies, but some goes to those who care for them, too.

First milk, the farmers call it, thick like blood, the color of a lily's stamen.

Ausma decides we will use it to make bread, so sweet there's no call for sugar, so thick it needs nothing else to bind the flour.

The radio is playing. Ausma sings along: *Oh my beautiful youth, come back to me. . . .*

She hands me her rolling pin, so I can take a turn at the dough.

What was it like for my sister, after she left us, during the war? Ausma asks suddenly.

Harijs, who has come in to get a glass of water, overhears Ausma's question.

Do you know how many times I should have died? he says.

Shh! Ausma says. Not now with that! I want to know this.

Did you come here from America by airplane or by boat? Harijs tries again.

You! says Ausma. Don't interrupt. Don't you have something to do outside?

In America, Harijs tries one last time, do you have the same sky?

This time, Ausma looks at me, too.

My grandmother always told me it was different, I say. And now that I'm here, I can see she was right.

What's different? asks Ausma.

The clouds feel closer here. Like you can touch them as they drift by.

I always used to think the sky was the same sky, wherever you went, Ausma says. But your grandmother wrote the same thing to me once: *All I want is to see Latvia's sky one more time before I die. . . .* This was when she was in the camps, I think. A letter that reached us years later, after she had already made it to America, and we had come back from Siberia.

Ausma returns to working the dough, as if she is done with the conversation, but I can tell by the force with which she uses the heel of her hand to fold it, then fold it again, that she is thinking about something, turning it over it in her head.

What I mean is, were the camps really so bad? she says at last. Maybe they had dysentery. But she had a place to sleep and food. It couldn't have been anything like what we had to live through. All of it. The war. Then my father's death. Me having to run the farm, all by myself. Then being sent away. She left me alone to carry the weight of it all—just a child. She was spared from the worst of it. Wasn't she?

———

She is the only person to hold my father following his birth. He does not feel his own father's touch. *Soldier,* she writes on the necessary paperwork, when asked her husband's occupation, and signs whatever needs signing by herself. Whether my grandmother believes then that to bear this alone is simply a temporary condition, soon to be remedied by a miraculous resolution to the war, in which her husband emerges not only unscathed but also unaccountable for having fought in an army under fascist command; or if she has begun to suspect, based on the whispered news of overwhelmed troops, breached borders and orders of retreat, that it is to be the new life to which she must become accustomed, she never utters her thoughts on this aloud.

My father is born as Russian aircraft hurl fire down on the German troops hunkered down in the marshlands surrounding Riga, their guns tatting against the bellies of the big, wailing planes that are known to their own soldiers as hunchbacks. Massive, lumbering things, bulge-eyed, narrow-snouted, said by Stalin to be as essential as air and bread.

As this due date had approached, Livija asked her sister to come to Riga to help her. But then word came that all civilian rail service within the country had stopped. Then the phones no longer sang, and when lifted from their cradles, screamed a silence louder than the sound of the planes horneting overhead.

When it is time, she turns to a friend—a fellow accountant at the bacon export factory where my grandmother works. She comes to look after Maruta while my grandmother is in the maternity ward.

Her name is Liene, a diminutive of the English name Helen.

She is a single woman, with no family. The time has passed for her to have children of her own. And this may be the start of it, a plan, building like the contractions that will send my grandmother outside to catch the streetcar to the maternity ward housed in a building in downtown Riga that will one day house the Soviet secret police.

Maybe Livija is the one who asks. Maybe Liene asks, once she has spent time caring for two-year-old Maruta. Either way, a decision is made. Whatever happens next, it will happen with Liene's help.

The Soviets are encircling the city. Outside my grandmother's apartment on Peace Street, the bombs wail day and night, matching the pitch of the baby's cries. As my grandmother tries to get him to latch, Liene offers to bring my grandmother food, whatever she can find or trade. The only other people on the streets seem to be refugees, column after column, bent backs dusted with ash. They trail goats and calves, along with stories of villages to the east and the north burned like spoiled crops, the destruction caused by not just the advancing Russian troops but also the retreating German armies, who would rather level everything than leave anything, even a wedge of bread, behind for their enemies to claim. At night the refugees' cook-fires burn in the city's parks and cemeteries.

Through the radio, word comes of each new town taken. Liepaja, Jelgava, Tukums, where it is said, people are flayed alive, women raped, a man's hand severed from his wrist by a Russian soldier who wanted his watch (in every town, there are stories of Russians killing for watches, so that it grows unclear whether we are talking about actual theft, or simply repeating a parable about the destruction of order, of certainty, of all previously agreed upon references).

Officers of the Reich can be seen racewalking Riga's narrow streets toward the port, where they descend gangplanks of ships bound back to Deutschland. The radio soothes—*avoid panic*—as the city flares. Soon the refugees' animals begin to disappear, reduced to nothing more than smears of fat, gristled bones. Then the refugees disappear, too. Some are down at the docks, begging for a spot on any departing boat. No room, they're told. That's because others are already on board, rounded up against their will by Riga's police, who are under order to find all able-bodied men and women who can be sent to the Reich to help try to reverse the course of the war, whether they want to or not. In the forests outside Riga, soldiers order the few Jewish prisoners not yet murdered to shove the lips of their shovels deep into the earth to exhume the bodies of those who have already been slaughtered. And then they make them burn the corpses, before they themselves are shot.

From the middle of September onward, Riga is bombed every night. No one sleeps. Or if they do, they sleep cocooned in clothing, shoes against the sheets, so that they are ready to run.

Maybe it is when the Germans girdle two of the bridges leading into Riga with explosives—what is a bridge if not the promise of passage—or maybe she has heard that soon they will start slipping mines into the waters around the port, but now leaving is all Livija can think about.

No matter what she chooses—to stay or to go—it will only promise more uncertainty. In the end, my grandmother chooses an uncertainty that she hopes, at least for the moment, will deliver her, and the children, from the immediate threat of violence, from the bombs spit by the hunchbacks that maim and crush, like the children a few blocks over, now entombed in the rubble of their apartment; from the gunfire of snipers who have taken position on bridges, on rooftops, drunk on vodka, some say, shooting at ghosts.

Out on the street, her friend Liene waits, pale eyes stinging for the smoke, one more set of hands for the babies. They attempt to board a boat out of Riga, jostled up the gangplank by the parade of groaning bags, swaddled bodies, layered not against cold, but to maximize the number of clothes one might carry, coats clinking, hems heavy with coin, fur stoles circling necks and shoulders like life rings. In the pocket of my grandmother's coat, the photos my grandfather has taken, freed from their albums to take up less space, a jumble now of baby, baby and sow, baby and switch, baby on horse, baby and mother, baby and father, now the mother on her own, seen not as parent, but as lover, face framed by the gentle V in a vase of fresh-cut pussy willows, her close-lipped smile coded, charged. They make it as far as the deck, but then are ushered off again to make room for retreating German troops. On the shore, they stand, numb, watching the boat's departure.

We can imagine from our own safe distance the water roiling in the ship's wake, like the surface of a pot left to boil too long. And then the familiar drone from the skies, a blink, and the sea explodes.

When they look again, the plane is gone, the boat is gone, the water still.

Years later, long after she is dead, and after I have begun my trips to her lost village, in a satchel tucked in the far corner of my grandmother's closet, I will find a ticket granting passage to a boat departing Riga's harbor on that day. I will never be able to determine whether this is the ticket for the lost ship that almost carried her, or if it was for the ticket of the boat she eventually boarded, and which ultimately spirited her from Latvia. Eventually, and it will take a long time, I will realize that it does not matter.

Either way, its presence serves to establish the same proof, and that is not of the idea of proof in the definite sense—that which is clear and determined and fathomable—but rather proof of all that can be explained only by random happenstance, a slight hesitation, a pause, a retraction, a stupid doubling back, action that unfolds without regard to intent; that there is nothing to your survival more grand than the ship you took, or did not take, that your claim on life is as thin as this ticket, the edges worried, shiny with the oils of her hand, as if she had taken it out and looked at it again and again.

WHAT DID she see once they made land, and began to walk, trying to make their way west? Hundreds of thousands of other people were doing the same: the displaced, deserters, war criminals, their intended victims who had managed to resist, to escape, all walking as one limping mass through the carnage. Likely she saw versions of what other people saw or said they saw: a teenage girl who stopped the flapping of her shrapnel-studded scalp with her last bobby pin; the man forced to slit the throat of his horse after it dropped to knees, as if its legs were broken at the fetlocks, and refused to rise, only to find moments later, strangers setting upon the steaming carcass with knives; the clots of smoke that hung over villages, the burning of unearthed bodies, the German troops and their local collaborators trying to erase all evidence of their killings; the silence of those who witnessed this, but never spoke of what they knew, trying to erase what they had not done; women, traveling alone, regardless of age, forced behind barns, into roadside copses by men in uniform, emerging, the backs of their skirts bloodied.

While alive, she chose to skip over this part of her trek, traveled it by way of omission, winding narrative detours. She told instead a few choice stories that reinforced chance, close calls. Close calls imply lack of agency. Lack of agency implies that you were powerless to react to what you saw.

She would limit her account to statements such as: *We slept in the woods during the day, and tried to keep the children quiet. Then we would walk at night.*

Why?

We did not want the soldiers to see us. That's all she would say. *Sometimes they would come close, and once I thought they would see the diapers we had put on the branches to dry, and I thought that was it, but they walked past us.*

In death, there is less circumspection, scraps of paper that do the talking for her, books that suddenly announce their presence in cabinets scanned a hundred times, and when their spines are cracked, reveal select pages dog-eared by her silent hand. Old tickets unslip themselves from hidden wallet sleeves.

These clues weave with the words she left, filling in some of the blank spaces on the map of her trek across Europe, the nine months she spent walking through territories that remained contested, territories where the last chaotic days of the war would unfold.

She mentioned once that she and Liene tried to follow the rail tracks, a common route for Europe's displaced at the time, one of the last intact paths that one could trace through the flattened landscape. She would have skirted Berlin while Hitler gophered underground, as the city above him flashed and cindered. She would have walked along tracks where railcars tried to shuttle concentration camp prisoners ahead of advancing Allied troops, to new places of death, or death, they hoped, along the way. She would have traveled through a landscape where it was not uncommon to find children wandering parentless among the columns of refugees, clothes still charred from the blast of the bomb that had somehow spared them, not yet old enough to recall the particulars of their names, no idea where they were going, simply absorbed by the blind forward momentum of so many people in motion, all of them trying to get somewhere, anywhere beyond the next air strike.

Sometimes, when they did not think they could walk another step, they tried to hop boxcars, Liene climbing first, Livija handing her the children, then clamoring after. They looked for farms, she told me, especially in winter, wisps of smoke, a chained cow. Sometimes, as soon as they could stop, they would hop down and double back. Cows meant they might be able to offer their help as milkers in exchange for something to eat, or even just a spare cup dipped in the pails for the children. Even when they did not understand what my grandmother was saying, the farmers recognized her hands. Usually, though, my grandmother let Liene talk, or if they could not be sure it was safe, she would wait in the bushes while Liene went ahead on reconnaissance. Liene spoke perfect German and so she could offer a cover, if needed, could pretend to be local. Sometimes a farmer might let Livija and Liene and the children stay a few nights in the barn, and, briefly, there were times, nestled in the hay, feeling the children's breath prick her neck, she might allow herself for a second to remember Gulbene, sleeping in the loft on the summer's hottest nights, each poke and scratch of the straw beneath her that released a smell like cobwebs in sunlight.

They woke to tendriled breath, the crackling of frost underfoot. When it was time to move on, they buttoned the children inside their coats, and hipped them through the wind. Ice rimed the puddles. They cracked it with their toes, dragged graying diapers through the slurry, and as they had done back home, hanging laundry outside, even in the dead of Latvia's winters, they waited for the fabric to freeze into stiff sheets— their signal that all the water had evaporated and the clothing was, in fact, dry.

When the baby boy cried because Livija had less milk for him than he knew there should be, Liene was the one who took him and bounced him, tried to soothe away hunger with silly songs. With her fingers, in forest light, under the cover of bird-song, she combed Maruta's rook-wing hair. For the children of Latvia, with its unceasing history of occupations and wars, famine and servitude, parents were forever being snatched away, and the old myths were full of stories of the role of the surrogate.

> Titmouse, chaffinch, where are your children?
> —Over on the other side of the Daugava,
> In the branch of an oak.
> But who rocks them?
> Who raises them?
> —Mother Wind rocks them.
> Mother Wind raises them.

Apple trees were said to be mothers to those who had none. Beneath their boughs lonely girls could go and feel the soft fall of petals as an acknowledgement of their tears. But what of the women, like Liene, who wanted to be mothers, but could not have children of their own? She spent nine months on the road with my father and my aunt, as long as if she could have carried her own baby to term, and she felt each child grow heavier in her arms.

She watched my father's features change from the squinting, blurry outlines of an infant to someone solid, intense, heavy-browed. He locked eyes with her, smiled at the sound of her voice. He was also growing harder to hold. He kicked, threw back his head, as if trying to make eye contact with the pilots in the planes always screaming overhead. The boy wanted to crawl, but they had to keep moving.

The women tried to stay away from the cities, the bloated carcasses trapped in the rubble, the flies, the detached hooves and scraps of hides turning sweet water sour, the living shitting uncontrollably.

Livija and Liene said they were tempted to stop only once, after they heard a rumor that they should try a city a bit farther to the east, where the train station had been turned over to refugees. Liene went ahead to look, while my grandmother and the children waited.

When Liene finally returned the next morning, she described the scene: the stench of the diesel engines, sulfur, the unwashed. Hundreds of people crammed onto the platforms, stowed in storage areas, like luggage, lying in the basement. There was absolutely no room, she said.

Then we keep moving, Livija said.

Later that night, when they stopped to look in the direction of where they had just been, when they looked back toward Dresden, they saw fire where there should have been sky.

They continued, slowly, to work their way north, tracing an arcing path clockwise, toward the sea, stopping first at Lübeck, then moving on to a DP camp in Pinneberg, on the outskirts of Hamburg. They stayed together as long as they could. But, eventually, Liene left—among the first refugees to be offered a chance to emigrate, in her case to England. Reluctantly, she left my grandmother and the children behind. She moved to London and married another Latvian refugee, a maker of traditional jewelry.

Decades later, when my father remarried, Liene's husband gave my stepmother a silver ring bearing a cascade of charms onto which he had hammered the ancient symbols calling forth things like health and joy, and also: fertility. And when my father and my stepmother had their first child, my little sister, they named her for this woman who helped carry my father through the worst of the war.

We went to visit my sister's namesake in London when my sister was just three months old and when Liene reached down to take her from her stroller for the first time, I can only imagine her body instinctively remembered what it was to hold my father at that age.

I could not sleep for the jet lag while we were there, and I remember once finding Liene sitting at the kitchen table in the middle of the night. She seemed to be crying. I was maybe ten years old at the time. She did not say anything, just fetched a glass jar of milk from the back step, its foil seal studded with tiny puncture marks from birds pushing their beaks through to reach the cream. She sloshed some milk from the bottle into a pan that she heated until it steamed, and then she sat with me, lost in thought, until I had emptied the whole mug. Then she walked me back to my bed and pulled the covers to my chin and placed a palm, soft from her years in the city, on the side of my face until I closed my eyes.

Years later, when she was at the edge of death, Liene wrote to my father, begging him to help her, to come to her.

Her husband was gone. It had not been a happy marriage. She was all alone now, in London, and she wanted him to know how she had thought of him as her son, too, in those days on the war roads, imagined for a brief while that he was her boy. He had given her a glimpse of what it was to be a mother, and she ached for him still.

He never wrote back. My father admitted this story to me only recently, and he wept as he told me.

It just felt too intense, he said. I'm so ashamed when I think about it now, that I let her down like that, but I just couldn't handle it. It frightened me. I didn't know how to respond in the face of all that . . .

He never finished his sentence that night, but the word I insert even now, as I replay our conversation, is *need*.

And here I mean *need* in its most ancient and basic sense. Not *need* as something soft or longing or wistful, but *need* as something anguished, howling, blood kin, even in etymology, to misery, to suffering, to anguish—*need* as linguistic ancestor to the Old English word for *trouble* or *pain*, but also: the Proto-Germanic word for *violence*.

Here I mean *need* as something that awakens us to that which causes us unendurable distress, but also: that which could help us abide it.

Need teaches us how to articulate that which could exist on the other side of our suffering, to give it a name.

But let's say it is your name that is spoken.

There's something intensely moving about that—to be called

in such a way. But there is also something frightening, too. Because now there is no way to separate yourself or your understanding of the depth of that person's need of you from the depth of the pain that summoned it.

When I tell Ausma what I have managed to piece together of my grandmother's journey, her months of flight, she says nothing at first. Just gets up, and starts to break kindling to start a fire in the kitchen stove for the bread.

Do you know what hurts the most? Ausma says at last. She struggles to speak, keeps her face to the fire. I needed her. But, from what you say, she needed me. All she went through. And now, my sister is buried so far from here, in strange soil. There's no way for me to go to her, to do something for her, even now.

Later that night, as I try to sleep, I will wonder whether the sounds I am hearing are coming from the barn, where the mother and her calves are now berthed in separate stalls, or from somewhere closer still.

XIV

THE NEXT TIME I come back to Latvia, it's winter, the cows' coats thick and draggly, as if in imitation of the hoarfrost that tinsels the trees each morning.

The local newspaper keeps its moon watch, says now—when the moon is old, as thin as a curl of fat—it is time to take saw teeth to trees. This way, the resulting wood will release the most heat. On the evening news, an astrologer is interviewed with the kind of seriousness one normally sees reserved for members of government. What can we expect in the year ahead? She advises everyone to spend more time in nature.

In the local paper, a story runs that more Latvian babies are being born abroad than in-country. What's a young person supposed to do, says Aivars, the husband of Ausma's daughter Ligita. Live next to all these abandoned farmhouses, falling down around him, with his hand on his heart, singing "God Bless Latvia"?

Their daughter, the mother of the two little girls, including the one who found the nest on my first visit, has recently moved to Norway.

The days are long and dark, with an edge of cold that sears the lungs. They send me to the sauna, where Aivars has strung camouflage netting outside, so that we can sit in the heat until we cannot bear it, then fling open the back door and plunge our steaming bodies in the old well to cool down. We jump feetfirst so our toes will crack the ice that seals the water's surface. I imagine, briefly, my grandmother Livija toeing frozen puddles in the flare-lit woods.

The puppy from my first visit is now so big his paws punch holes in the snow as large as tea saucers, and he serves as personal escort to each steaming streaker. He stands at the well's edge and greets us with jubilant barks when we shoot back up to repierce the iced surface, screaming without sound for the shock of the cold, our lungs learning to heave air again, as if reborn.

One day, he will run into the woods, trailing cheeky curls of breath like he has swallowed one of Aivars's cigarettes, and never come back.

When this happens, Ligita will go to the neighbor, the man who sees things, the man who everyone agrees can use a stick to find well water where no one else can. He tells her that the puppy is dead, that he tangled with something ferocious and wild, and he tried, with all the strength he had, to get back to them, but he was too hurt, and couldn't drag himself home. The neighbor who sees things describes the exact spot where the dog's body lies in the snow, but one part of the forest can look so much like the next in winter, and so there is nothing to do but accept another disappearance.

I draw an "x" in the fog of the car window the next time we drive past the pine at the crossroads that once marked the way to the old cemetery.

One morning, I wake up sick, shivering. Probably from

being too reckless with the sauna and the well. Everyone agrees I may have invited a chill into my body. Ligita, who also sees things, though mostly in her dreams—A witch! Aivars says in a way that you can tell is joking and maybe not joking all at once—makes me inhale the smoke from a burned thread of linen.

Aivars follows with a shot of balsam. One for him, too, *so you won't be lonely.* And then one more all around, *so that we favor each leg equally.*

THIS IS THE WINTER Ausma's wood-fired furnace stops working. The pages of her gardening magazines kept stacked next to the Christmas cactus freeze together, and the cats refuse to come out from under the cow barn. Above them, the layer of hay upon the stall floors, the wet heat of the cows' urine, affords at least some insulation.

We huddle in the kitchen around the wood-burning stove, normally used for baking, wearing all our clothes, hats and mittens. Ausma knits me a pair of wool socks. Do you know how many times I should have died? Harijs asks, his voice visible in the air between us. But this time, he cannot remember times two and five without prompting. Later Ausma tells me he has started to confuse the day of the week, the year, to talk of memories from their life together that could not have happened.

And still the paper asks its jokes:

Son: Mama, why do you always stand by the window when I sing?

Mother: I don't want people to think that I am hitting you. . . .

———

THE FIRST THING she saw when they finally reached the other side of the sun: nothing. The landscape told her nothing. The sky was white. The ground was white. White as the piles of boiled bones her grandfather kept in his tannery shed. White as the linen threads Ausma used to weave the sheets she imagined she would one day spread on her wedding bed, but which instead were now flapping on a neighbor's clothesline, muttering Ausma's initials to the wind—AS, AS, AS.

They stepped off the train into a void, her brother, Janis, hopping on one leg, the other taken first by gangrene, then a prison doctor's saw, his crutches puncturing the scabbed and crusted top layer of winter's storms. Even when it was clear the Soviets had won, Janis had fought along with what remained of the Latvian Legion for seven months, backed into the westernmost edge of Latvia, refusing to give up. When finally they surrendered to the Russians, they were all taken as prisoners of war, sentenced to a labor camp outside of Moscow, on the way to Leningrad. There, his leg was crushed when the coal mine in which he had been working collapsed. They had allowed him to return home, only after the doctors had insisted he would not live long anyway. I guess I got better so they could send me to Siberia and kill me a second time, he said.

Her mother, Alma, followed slowly behind, trying to match her daughter's steps, as Ausma cleared a path for her through the snows.

They had thought it so cold inside the boxcar, the three of them trying to huddle under the single blanket Ausma had brought from the farm, watching through the slats as all color was leached from the passing land. There were others who had even less, who had come with only the clothes they were wearing, bare feet inside their boots. But this cold was like nothing they had ever known, like something wounded, ferocious with misery and pain. Later, the cold would try to take them as they walked, swallowing them in drifts that reached to their rib cages, smothering the breath from their chests, reaching into their pockets, filling them with snow. It would try to take them in their sleep, crawling into their beds, reweaving the strands of their blankets with ice. It stole their food, rendered it inedible, lifted the skin from their tongues, turned cheeks and the tips of noses the color of singed earth.

This was what waited for them after nearly three weeks of travel, packed into a single railcar, the space necessary for each person calculated by one particularly poetic bureaucrat to be *no larger than a grave*. Bog lands, unending steppes, burred and smothering forest. Blank lands. Areas in Russia's remote east, unpopulated, unnamed, unacknowledged on any map.

Although no one ever explicitly said their destination was Siberia, nor gave any explanation what this was about, Ausma knew, from the first round of deportations she had witnessed almost eight years ago, at thirteen, where they were headed, and that they were being sent there because someone somewhere for some reason wanted them banished to a place from which they could not come back.

She was a special exile now, her passport confiscated, a form presented for her to sign—*I have chosen to relocate of my own volition and will never return to the region I previously occupied: I will live out the rest of my days in the area where I have volunteered to be assigned*. Then her paperwork was dated 1949, stamped *strictly secret*, treated, outwardly, as if it never existed, and archived—along with 41,000 other files, known collectively to those involved in the planning and execution of this mass exile by its code name: *Operation Tidal Wave.*

IT FELT STRANGE to walk again, after so long on the train, its juddering still echoing through Ausma as she helped her mother and brother toward the processing center, a crude, sprawling compound of barrackslike buildings where they were told to prepare for the selection, although no one explained exactly what that meant.

Still echoing inside them: collective memories of the journey east, which held the goatlike cries of an elderly man, all alone, saying the name of his daughter, or his wife or his mother, no one knew, over and over again until it sounded like one continuous trilling of a single vowel, EEEEEEEEE; the woman who wet herself rather than perch on the slick lip of the hole which served as the latrine for the entire car, steam rising from her lap afterward, until someone next to her, wanting to maintain at least a symbolic privacy, snuffed it with a coat; the cups of soup handed out at the depots where the trains would stop, potato skins floating in tepid broth, chased with a swallow of what tasted like water in which fallen leaves had stewed for days; and the tiny bundle leaving the guard's hand.

What the mother of the baby did after the guard took her dead child, Ausma does not recall, or does not want to recall. So she chooses silence instead.

I don't think she made a sound. There was more quiet than you would think.

Once, seen through the slats, along the rail lines: a corpse, possibly, someone tossed from a different Siberian transport, a perfect silhouette left untouched by teeth or beaks. Glimpsed

through the slats, the body looked disconcertingly like someone who had simply stopped after a long trek and lay down
momentarily to consider the sky.

But there was this, too; I shouldn't forget this:

The local Russians who ventured up to the railcars at some
of the smaller stops, mittening weeviled bread through the
open doors, extending pails of water.

How quickly the scene cuts from cruelty to kindness, and
it is clear that this is how she experienced it, how it felt at the
time, a bewildering, contradictory series of encounters that
confused kindness and pain. I see the same themes emerge in
the accounts of others who were taken on the same transport
as Ausma, from the same village, on the same day, transcripts
of survivors' oral histories that I have begun to collect from
any written account I can find. Taken together, read one after
another, the voices become a kind of communal dirge, a strange
polyphony of memories and fears and wonderings that speak
at once to the collective experience of suffering, and to no one's
experience but their own:

> When we stepped off the train, the first thing I saw was
> carts, pulled by oxen, and they loaded the sickest people
> in the back, those who could no longer stand, and ordered
> the rest of us to fall in behind.

> The barracks where they took us first had been built to
> hold German prisoners of war. That's what I was told.
> They had been built hastily, with green wood, so there
> were gaps in the walls and the floors, as the wood wept all
> its moisture, then shrank.

There were people who grew tired quickly—we had eaten so little for days—and sometimes someone dropped to the ground, but we were told we couldn't stop for them.

What I want to know is why did our guards have guns? Where were we going to run?

When the ice melted, I saw them take bodies and drop them in the lake.

Someone said they heard that we would be presented to the local collectives, as soon as the ice broke on the river, and they would take turns picking us, like one picks a cow. The weakest would be sent to the worst places, so they might die quicker. You didn't want to go where the invalids and the elderly went. I went and found berries to crush and rub on my cheeks, so I would look like someone healthy, someone they wanted to choose.

THEY WERE among the last to be chosen. Not the very last. But close to the last.

First, the eyes of the collective's officials had fallen on the space where her brother's leg should have been. Next, the members of the collective studied Ausma's mother, Alma, her face withered beneath her kerchief, like the surface of an apple, forgotten beneath the tree, left to the workings of the wasps and the ants and the rain.

It was clear that the two of them would be useless to contribute to the required work quotas. Then they saw Ausma.

Ausma, the girl who had spent the last four years since her father's death running the family farm because her brother was too damaged, her mother too weak with sickness and grief, her sister lost to the war roads, they had no idea where.

There was no one left but this girl, who had abandoned the idea of school or dances or courting to rise at three each morning to milk the cows and ration the hay that she alone had scythed and turned and dried and wagoned back to the loft, day after day as summer transitioned to fall, until her hands turned black with blood.

The fabric of her dresses—now thin and shiny at the back, stretched and strained by the thickening of her shoulders, the hardening of her body. Like stone, she thought, not wood. She felt the grinding of her joints whenever she raised her arms to swing an axe or to wrap a calving chain around one of the cows' reluctant births.

They saw in her the entire story of the past four years: she could do the work of all three.

A woman stepped up to Ausma, her hands encased in what looked like fur from a dog, something with an angry, wiry pelt, with what looked like tooth scars, tar-colored welts, running beneath the fur, like veins.

The woman spoke, her voice low, expressionless, formal.

Ausma didn't speak Russian, and she couldn't pull any meaning from the woman's tone.

The woman began to walk away, then turned and indicated that Ausma and her brother and mother should follow.

It wasn't until much later that Ausma finally learned what the woman had said that day. But not until after they had moved into a corner of the woman's kitchen, in a small shack at the edge of a collective farm, a place named for the Russian word for *flame*, where for half the year, milk left in a pail for more than five minutes would freeze; after the woman had taught Ausma her first Russian word, *chai*, a word which in normal circumstances meant tea, but in this new world meant boiled water with a lashing of milk, skimmed with a spoon from one of the frozen pails; after Ausma had gathered the woman's story—that she had lived in Siberia for decades, had survived famines that had killed everyone else around her.

She'd said: *I am sorry this has happened to you.*

XV

WHEN I was still in college, working for a paper in Albuquerque for the summer, I once took a man's life from him as his sister listened.

What I mean is that I had been assigned to work the newsroom's predawn shift, lone monitor of the scanners and phones and faxes, ready to catch any possible emergencies that might happen when the rest of the world was still deep in sleep. Mostly, it would be quiet, supervisors assured me. But early in my assignment, I received a call from the local police department: a man murdered after an altercation outside a bar. They gave me his name and date of birth. This was newsworthy, the supervising editor told me, when I sketched the details for him; we had just enough time to get something in the first edition, if I got to work.

And so I began to do what I had been trained to do, to call those who might know the man, who might, using language borrowed from one veteran reporter, *help me provide readers with a portrait of your loved one, help make him more than a name and a victim.*

I located a number of someone who shared the man's surname, and dialed.

A woman answered.

I was sorry to bother her so early, I said. But I was looking for the family of ——?

That's my brother, she said. He'd been staying with her, she explained, but he was out right now.

And then she paused, as if letting her words and the implication of them in this context catch up with each other. What's happened? she said.

That's when I knew that police had not yet informed the family of this man's death. It was an unheard-of breach of protocol. Police departments never released to the press the name of someone who had died until family had been informed first. But something had clearly broken down on this night.

You should call the Albuquerque police, I tried, but the woman was yelling now—*What's happened to my brother*—no longer a plea, but an insistence.

At some level she knew, and it was as if she wanted me to do the right thing, even if it was the most hurtful thing, wanted me to get it over with, because she didn't want me to let her imagine for another second that this could be anything other than the horror she suspected.

He was killed, I said. Outside a bar.

And I still remember the sound she made, then the sound of a phone falling, the click of my own handset, the way I hated myself for summoning just enough momentary numbness to write something that reflected none of the ugliness of what had just happened, but not enough to be unmoved by praise from my editor for my *good work*.

I had left no record of my cruelty, only a clean, compelling narrative about pain, as it is suffered and inflicted upon others.

Ausma does not seem to want to talk anymore.

It's summer now, a new visit.

She does not say as much to me. She is so grateful to have the presence of her sister restored to her life through me, that she will suffer my questions, endure the details that I am keen to write down to *fill in the details of our family story.* She does not correct me, never says, don't you mean your story?

Because both of us know this has become my story, a story I am constructing from her stories, her words, her memories, to try to answer something for myself, something I don't know how to reach, except through her. But it is a story Ausma does not want anymore. She abandoned it years ago, walked away and left it to rot like the remains of Lembi.

So she simply stops speaking.

She will walk away suddenly. Will go outside. And quietly remove the chain from the dog that charges anyone who does not live at the house. The dog that has bitten at least five people, I will discover later, including a man who came to fix the telephone. Once, while helping Harijs in the barn, I wandered too close, and he lunged to the end of his tether and snapped the air in front of my nose.

The dog watches me through the window, guarding me now from leaving the house. I move from room to room, so that I might see what Ausma is doing: scattering scraps for the chickens, dragging a hoe down her rows of potatoes, culling softened turnips from the bins in the cold cellar. The dog moves whenever I move. I nap. I reread my notes. I open the door to try to call to Ausma to tie him up so I can go outside and help her with chores, but I make it as far as the porch before the dog charges. Always, a few hours later, Ausma returns. And I know that this means that questions are over for the day. It is our truce.

One night, as we are watching an old Latvian movie from

the 1980s, a period drama set in Siberia, she is suddenly animated, commenting on the sets, their accuracy, linking what she sees to her own memories. So I think I might attempt to ask her more questions, draw out just a few more details, and I imagine that I am being delicate, keeping things light, but I can feel her growing smaller and smaller, pulling into herself, until finally she is no smaller than the spot that remains at the center of the screen of the old television, which she has shut off midprogram. Time for bed, she says.

The next morning, I go for a run while it is still dark, past rye fields and barley fields and down mud-dried roads where I must occasionally stop for a procession of cows; through the nearby village where lightning recently struck and split a linden tree in which storks had nested, making the front page of the local paper: "Baby Storks Crushed."

I have made it a point to never leave the house until I know the dog is tied, and they have been good about keeping him restrained until I return.

But as I come up the path to Ausma's house, I see the dog's empty lead coiled in the dirt. I spot Harijs, outside the barn, and I wave my hands, hoping to alert him—and not the dog—to my presence. He manages to understand my pantomime and fishes his finger under the dog's collar to hold him as I slip inside.

I freed him, says Ausma, when I mention the dog was loose. I feel so bad for him tied up all day. Like a prisoner. Besides, he knows you are living here now. He knows you are family.

Later that afternoon, when I go to visit one of Ausma's granddaughters, who lives just up the hill, I double-check that the chain still holds a dog. The evening is warm, like new milk, the locals say.

I sit with Ausma's granddaughter on a bench carved from a log, in view of the cows that have been turned out to graze for the night. Ausma's granddaughter tells me which cows love people, will follow them like dogs, nuzzling hands, licking faces, which are slow or slightly touched and need the others to remind them of their stalls, which can be coaxed with heels of bread. She recites the names of every cow she has loved. As I walk back down the hill drunk on the summer air and the strange sweetness of the conversation, a recitation of cows, I register movement out of the corner of my eye, something slipping soundlessly from behind a stand of filbert trees.

And I have only enough time to register this fact when I feel a pinch and burn and my leg gives, as the dog sinks a tooth in my calf.

XVI

ONCE, LONG AGO, in the region of Latvia where my grandmother is from, there was a man named Thies who for a time, before he came into his true calling, lived as a beggar.

One day, a man approached the beggar Thies. How about a drink, the man said, and Thies, given his current situation, could see no reason to decline. Back and forth the men passed a jug between them, feeling the edges of themselves blur. The man offered to make a toast to Thies, to which Thies had no objection. Maybe it would change his fortunes. When the man had finished, he raised the jug as if to take a nip, but instead blew through his lips into its neck—three exhalations. *You will become like me*, he whispered, before placing the vessel back in Thies's hands, and waited for him to drink.

And that's how you became a werewolf? asked one of the judges, who had hauled Thies in for questioning.

Yes, said Thies. He didn't pause or stutter or hesitate.

It was the year 1691. By this time, Thies was in his eighties and had been werewolfing for most of his life.

His neighbors confirmed his assertion.

Everyone knows Thies is a werewolf, they said. They stated it matter-of-factly, the way someone would state a thing everyone knows: cows have a hard time eating thistle, or, storks hiss.

And just what does one do, when one is a werewolf? the judges wanted to know.

Well, Thies said, at certain times of year, he and his other werewolf friends shed their clothing and assumed the form of wolves.

What then?

They ate farm animals, sometimes. Mostly they traveled to hell—which could be reached through a swamp located about a twenty-kilometer walk from the village. They went to hell to retrieve the people's blessings of their crops that had been stolen by wizards and delivered to the devil. Sometimes, this resulted in battles. This past year, he had managed to slip into hell and retrieve barley, oats and rye, which meant there would be a good harvest come fall.

So you admit that you consort with the devil, the judges pressed.

No, insisted Thies. He and the other werewolves worked against the devil. Maybe a better way to describe them, he said, was *hounds of god*.

But do you go to church and say your prayers?

Thies had to confess that he did not. He was an old man, and these were things that were beyond his capacity to understand. Who knew where souls went?

All he knew was that since he had turned into a werewolf, he knew how to say just the right words in just the right way, so that he could send his words to hell, too, *to fetch back the soul that the devil has taken*, and in this way, he would raise sick horses and cows from the floors of their stalls, unwither failing crops.

Yes, his neighbors agreed, Thies was a healer of considerable reputation, who could use the same words that you or I would use, regular words, but he could arrange them in such a way as to stop a cut's weeping or to chase wolves from the woods.

On the subject of what the judges meant and what Thies meant when they each said the same word *werewolf*, this would never be satisfactorily resolved in court that day.

Did Thies truly believe that he could assume another's form, or was he saying, in his own way, with regular words, arranged in just the right order, that imagination can also be its own form of transcendence, a kind of survival?

Thies would never get another chance to explain.

The judges had reached a verdict.

As they saw it, Thies and his words were dangerous and confusing, and the words needed to stop. And the only way they could see to stop him and stop his words from spreading any further within the village was to forever separate him from the context of his stories, to render Thies and his words, placeless.

AND SO it came to pass that they were now living in the days that followed the war's end, the days of placelessness, when more than 30 million people had been scattered across Europe and had lost their words for home. All of them insisting, for wildly different reasons, that they could no more return to where they had just come than bombs can be undropped; than numbers on arms could be uninked; than death sentences for collaborating with the enemy—not because you believed in fascism but only because you wanted so badly to stop communism—could be unissued. No more than the shame could be unfelt that sometimes squirms its way to the surface of your waking thoughts before you manage to push it back down, the things you did or perhaps just as much the things you did not do that privileged you and your survival over anyone else's, that meant you ignored another's visible suffering.

The same shorthand was used to refer to all of them: DPs, as in Displaced Persons. An estimated 200,000 to 250,000 Latvians fled for the West during the war years; of that number, more than 100,000 were ultimately forced to make the trip back—because they were recaptured by the Soviets or returned by Western forces. That left about 120,000 Latvians who remained DPs. They took the acronym and used its letters to construct an alternate term for themselves: Dieva Putnini. Dieva from dievs, as in the Latvian god of sky. Putnini as in the diminutive for bird. *Little birds*. As in that which is ungrounded; as in that which can foretell sorrow, but also possibly hope; as in being in an endless state of passage.

When finally, my grandmother and my father and Liene and Maruta passed through the steel gates of Camp 269 UNRRA Pinneberg, where 3800 of the placeless, mostly Latvians, had been assigned temporary shelter, my father had only just found his capacity for speech, the ability to name himself and the things around him—*little bird*; *lost boy*.

At night, curled in on himself, as if making himself as small as possible to give others more room, my father, the baby who had absorbed the flight paths of the bombers from his mother's arms, and from Liene's arms, now dreamed in a barracks that had billeted young Luftwaffe pilots.

Where once they had absorbed lessons in the principles of aerodynamics and aerospace engineering, and how to navigate by the position of the stars, he now played on the floor with scraps of paper that he made glide and twitch with his breath as if they could take wing.

It was a life defined by waiting, wherever you found yourself, whether assigned to scratchy cots wedged inside stalls that until recently berthed saddle horses for the German cavalry or boarded in bunks installed in former surgical suites that still smelled faintly of amputations, cauterized wounds. Mothers approached toddlers in their rooms, absorbed in quiet play, only to discover them gumming what looked like scraps of exploded ordnance. Those early days passed in an endless stretch of unstructured hours, the monotony of small temporary rooms.

Together, they were cleansed in clouds of DDT, the babies sometimes laughing into the fog, trying to catch it in their mouths like snowfall, the women instructed to kneel slightly, as if in curtsey, and to lift the hem of their skirts just enough to accommodate the delouser's nozzle, with its puff of air and the fine dusting that would drive away the lice and their typhus. For hours afterward, each step, each brush of one thigh against the other, would release the chemical's smell—hints of burned marzipan. No, others said, more like borscht.

Lice were not the only named fear.

Also: dysentery, rickets, diphtheria, syphilis, TB, scabies, polio.

They learned to surrender themselves for regular medical inspections, passed their health record books to the nurses and doctors to initial without thought for privacy, their lives now a running count of coughs and infections, lung spots and fevers. On the days of the mass inoculations—hundreds of the camp's children injected at once, the nurses punching the flesh of one twitching buttock after another—the mothers helped skin their babies from their chunky wool tights. Rabbit pants, the Latvians called them.

But for all the shots, sickness still found them.

One morning, Livija lifted Maruta from sheets sweated wet.

In time, they would learn she had contracted polio. But on that day, all they knew was the force of her fever, that she was listless, unable to sip water without distress.

A nurse came, and perhaps thinking it was something that could be cured with a dose of antibiotics, she decided to administer a shot, a quick punch and wriggle of the rabbit's haunch.

Whether out of haste or ignorance, or both, she chose to slip the needle into the center of Maruta's buttock, and pierced her sciatic nerve.

Almost immediately, Maruta's leg on that side went limp, the ankle flopping as if attached to the foot by a thin tongue of skin.

Between this, and the effects of the polio, Maruta would ultimately struggle to take a single step, her legs bound in braces, pushing a walker.

And, eventually, though still years in the future, but already starting then, in the camp—as she tried, and failed, to grasp the hands of the other small children whose mothers encouraged them to circle up in the weak sun to sing and dance as a distraction from the guard towers and the phlegm-colored soup and the fact that they were swaddled not in diapers but in flyers instructing the refugees on the regulations of the camp—the muscles of all four of her limbs started to shrink, atrophying, until one day, which would mark the beginning of her last days, the only comfortable place for her was bed.

These were the unnamed fears:

That you—you were the reason this happened.

That you were the one to blame.

That the moment you pushed the door closed on your former life, the moment you took to the road, chose flight over your family and the farm—all the while telling yourself that you were making the right choice, the only choice—you might have been mistaken.

And now this: your little boy, his sudden not-speaking, like an envelope quietly sealing itself shut.

WHAT DID my father understand of their life among the placeless? He would have been too young to remember the walls of the refugee processing centers that they passed through, covered with the names of family members whose whereabouts were unknown, sometimes a photo, if photos had come with the refugees: *Have you seen* —— *?*

But he most likely heard the nightly broadcasts that played on the camp radio, the voices of children, old enough to recall their names and from where they had come, sending their words out in search of lost parents. Perhaps he even understood the pitch of their pleas, if not the actual meaning.

Did he know his own father was missing, like so many of the men who were there, but weren't there, a number written then crossed out on their wives' intake forms?

He turned one, then two, before he even learned what the word *father* meant, at least what it meant in relationship to his own life, the shape that it occupied, its silence, save for the scrape of rough hands jacketing you for a trip outside, the impatient clapping tempo of a walk too fast for small legs, the crusting of one weeping eye.

On the subject of where Emils had been for the last two years, and what had happened to him in the war, he appeared to have drawn a line through his memories, as if he were a document from which hundreds of pages had suddenly been redacted. But the rage that sometimes gripped him and filled the little room that they shared—that rattled the tins of dried milk and sardines and sent rolling from the table the cigarettes that came in the refugees' boxes of rations, and which everyone traded on the black market for the things they really needed, like soap and sewing supplies—said enough for his family to suspect that he'd never really returned from wherever it was he'd gone.

What he did not say:

After the doctors had picked the bone fragments from the hole in his head and sutured it shut, then fitted the pit of his skull's orbit with an eye made of glass, after my grandfather had finally emerged from the coma induced by his injuries, the German military hospital in which he recuperated was seized by the Allies.

At this point, my grandfather was transferred to a prisoner-of-war camp in Belgium, where the Allies tried to make sense of men who wore the uniforms of Nazis, but who claimed that they were not Nazis at all, only conscripts, forced to join the army of their occupier. There were interrogations, and inside those interrogation rooms, if the stories of the men who were held there can be believed, the kinds of reckonings that accompany war's end, the release of collective anger and rage and fear.

In the end, after months of questioning, Allied investigators ruled that he was not a criminal, and let him go. But from the larger moral question of what constitutes collaboration, he would never be released.

Once again, my grandmother corrected her calculations, restoring the original *number of family members* to include her husband, but only because there was no other way to record the presence of someone who was back, but not back. He was not her first experience with a lost love, but she had learned the first time, at the tip of a nail, not to expect too much. And so, when her second lost love returned to her, she understood that she should be grateful for whatever remained—the skin laced fine with keloids, the lumbering pace, the square jaw grinding, always grinding, awake or asleep.

She had heard enough resurrection stories, myths that celebrate the possibility of regeneration—the revivification of those assumed dead—to know that there is almost always a hidden cost, almost always something that is held back in exchange for the right to return from the other side.

When he spoke, his voice sounded like the tip of a match drawn across phosphorus.

Mostly, he didn't speak.

He could disappear at any moment, even as he lay right beside her. She could feel him scuddering about inside himself, traveling years and miles, before abruptly returning to their bed to look at her in a way that told her she might be the only thing tethering him to this room, to her, to the two children asleep on their cots at their feet.

My grandmother listened to him breathe himself back to calm, the four of them suspended in the night-sounds of the barracks, the sound of secrets uncontained, slipping through the loose weave of the blankets hung as partitions, between the suitcases stacked in imitation of walls: who is loving whom, who is striking whom, who is sick on homebrew, who neglects their children, who calls out in their nightmares, and who thrashes in silence.

Like this, she would remind him without words. Being alive is like this.

A year after my grandfather's return, my grandmother gave birth to another child, a boy. This time, my grandfather was there to hold his second son.

Now, with a brother, my father began to find his voice again, to whisper to him, to tell him all he thought he should know about their home, its secrets and wonders and dangers: the puddles of oil and floating garbage at the camp's periphery that could be lanced with sticks; the older boys who stole and fought and ran from the police, and who once blamed my father for their supposed crimes when an officer stopped to talk to them, so that my father ran, too, and burrowed beneath a mattress for a very long time before he realized, in a pinioning of confusion and fear, that no one was looking for him at all.

By now, most of the refugees had lived nearly three years in circumstances meant only ever to be temporary. On the question of where the hundreds of thousands in Europe displaced by war should go next, the rest of the world had remained decidedly silent. Only Great Britain, Australia and Canada had come forward offering to help in any substantive way—*Where would you be willing to be resettled?* a form from that period had asked; *Canada,* my grandfather had written, his handwriting less certain than his answer—but even still, restrictions were such that all available spots would likely go only to young single men and women.

Few countries seemed to want resettle families with small children, let alone families who might be supporting someone with a disability, the war-maimed, the chronically ill, the elderly.

In the United States, Congress shut down all attempts to relocate any refugees, citing possible *shortages of housing and consumer goods, fear of reconversion unemployment, and apprehension as to the type of persons who were inmates of the D.P. camps in Europe.*

And in this way, the impermanent became mistaken for the indefinite.

Life in the indefinite was to scale piles of war rubble for sport, to root through the grit for anything that could be turned into toys, fragments of magnet, webs of cloth, unburned books, miraculously, once, a spoon.

It was to push donated baby dolls in donated baby carriages across reclaimed fields that had originally been graded to accommodate soldiers for inspection; to run naked on your mother's orders so that the sun on your bare skin might somehow help unbow the bend to your legs, unthicken the bones in your wrists that had begun to bulge beneath the skin, the first signs of rickets.

It was to pretend the smears of guts and grease in the barracks' basement were not from the pig reported stolen from a nearby farm. It was to see nothing when seeing nothing was required, as if you, too, had rinsed your gums with some of the black market liquor that was said to sometimes cause blindness.

Life in the indefinite was to leave the adults to meetings where they argued over the preservation of the language, the loosening of grammar, the loss of the old words for things that had no equivalent in this new life. They should resist becoming like potatoes with old eyes, one former farmer put it, never to be replanted.

So they searched for a word that would embody the state of remaining ready for the possibility of return, even as they prepared for the unlikelihood that they could ever go back.

By day they completed questionnaires and enrolled in English lessons and submitted themselves to certification tests so that they could prove themselves skilled at something—sewing, or typing, or factory work—anything that might convince a potential host nation that they were worthy of sponsorship, ready to contribute in any way needed. At night, they danced in folk collectives, taught their children the words to the old national anthem and organized choir recitals where the song begging the wind to carry them back to Latvia became the exiles' new unofficial anthem.

They hacked gardens from the fields where soldiers once drilled so that they could follow along with the seasons, as they would have back home, marking each day not in the usual increments of time, but by what is growing or what is not growing or what will soon grow.

And the chemists who had fled with the contents of their laboratories unable to bear the thought of leaving their life's work behind—Florence flasks and Bunsen burners, test tubes and crucible tongs; the librarians who arrived with armloads of their treasured first editions; the members of the national theater company who unlocked suitcases to reveal wigs and costumes; the printer who unloaded a working press—they all began to share their passions with their campmates. They published newspapers and printed books, such as the saga of Bear Slayer, his Black Knight now decidedly Russian.

The former academics re-created their lesson plans, hosting night classes for the refugees in their native languages—art history and folklore, statistics and physics—so many classes that the academics would eventually open their own university. Among the faculty of the new Baltic University, as it was called: my grandfather, the former economics professor, his old formulas awakening in him once more.

Lektor, he noted on his camp papers, wherever occupation was required, and inside the family's small room, he took to stacking all the books he could find that might be relevant to his classes—Adam Smith's *An Inquiry into the Nature and Causes of the Wealth of Nations*, *Self-Administration in England and Wales*, *Statistics I* in English, which he read with the help of a dictionary, given to him by one of the British officers who were running the camp.

Before long, he was named Chair of Economic Theory, and the family was walled in on all sides—as they ate, or as the adults made love with their hands over each other's mouths so the children wouldn't hear, or as they fought, or told the children not to fight by books offering concrete theories as to how and why people make the choices they do.

In this way, the camp residents gave themselves jobs when there were none, but for the lecturing and the farming and the dancing and the singing, they received no salary. Occasionally there were tasks to be done around the camp for what amounted to pocket money, never much.

Still, sometimes it was enough pocket money that you might decide, maybe, today, to bake something sweet—enough money anyway, to send your boys in search of a lemon.

Lemons aren't very sweet, said my father, once they were outside.

Let's get candy instead, said his little brother.

No, let's get an orange, said my father. Oranges are better.

Yes, agreed his brother, an orange will be a much better surprise than a lemon.

It was their first attempt at a present.

She did not scold them, merely set aside what she had started of the dough, then quartered the orange, and let the smell of the pith fill the room, as if this, too, could be a kind of celebration.

THERE WERE other outings:

Once, with their father, to the market just outside the camp in search of a fish that could feed all five of them.

The boys insisted on one so fresh they could see his gills still bellowing, pleading.

As they walked back to camp, the fish wrapped loosely in newspaper, the boys began to beg: Please, can we put him in the bathtub to see if he will swim?

Their father wasn't having it. This fish was to eat.

Besides, the bathtub was not theirs to put fish in as they pleased, he told them. They shared it with all the other residents on their barracks' floor.

They begged all the way home.

Finally, he gave in to them. But only for an hour, he said. And then it's dinner.

But then an hour became a day and a night and another day, and soon they were all listening for the sound of approaching footsteps, then rushing ahead to slam the communal bathroom door shut, so they could scoop the fish from the bathtub and into a pail, ridding the emptied basin of his roping strands of shit, his errant scales.

All yours, they would say, trying not to slosh the water as they carried the pail back to their room.

It wasn't long before word spread of the fish finning back and forth in the barracks bathtub. But rather than insist on its removal, everyone seemed charmed by the presence of the unlikely pet. Soon, all the bathers were transferring the fish to its pail while they washed, then sloshing him back over the lip of the tub when they'd finished.

They took to filling their bathrobe pockets with crumbs, chumming the water with bits of stale bread, encouraging the fish to rise, to mouth watery nonsense in their direction, fish-speak for good morning, or thank you, or you will find him soon, or she says she forgives you for not saying good-bye, or you will leave this place very soon, or whatever it was they imagined they needed to hear in order to get through this next day.

One of the little boys in the barracks thought he heard the fish say, Help me. I'm tired. I want to keep swimming.

So he went and found a knife and pressed the point into the fish's back, nudging him along.

Again, the fish said. Again. Thank you. I'm so tired, I've forgotten how to move.

What are these marks on your back, the bathers asked, watching the fish lurch into his pail, turning like a capsized boat to show his bleached belly, taking much too long to right himself again.

I just wanted to help, the boy said, when the fish stopped moving altogether, his eyes clouded over, the color of old fat pooled in the bottom of the pan, his back stippled with gashes. He seemed so quiet. I was trying to help make sure he wasn't dead.

MARUTA IS missing.

From these stories. From their daily lives.

When her polio infection was eventually diagnosed, she was sent to the nearest hospital, outside the camp, kept for months in the children's ward, where, at the time, it was thought that it be would be disruptive to the young patients' recovery and rehabilitation if their parents visited too often.

They were barred from seeing her for more than a few hours each weekend. They arranged for day passes, walked stiffly through the camp gates, past the guards, silently preparing themselves for this endless reenactment of separation, her tears, her building rage. They are losing her, even though the nurses comment on her progress. She will not look at them, tries to roll herself so that she faces the wall. As if she has decided it is somehow less painful to imagine they never came, because then, at least, she would not have to watch them leave her here, all by herself, again and again.

BACK AT the camp, they watched family after family leave.

Their number now just a few hundred refugees: the old, the broken, those whose bodies did not work in the ways a sponsoring nation tends to deem of use.

Grudgingly, the United States had begun to reconsider its earlier *apprehension as to the type of persons who were inmates of the D.P. camps in Europe.* And favored, in the end, were those refugees who could work as farmhands in the country's Midwest and its South, their prospects debated in such publications as *Congressional Quarterly*, a kind of scouting report for refugees:

> In Iowa, where the population has declined by 83,000 since 1940, a state survey showed that several thousand displaced persons could be welcomed there immediately. Kentucky is estimated to have a capacity to absorb over 5,000. In Minnesota Gov. Youngdahl's commission, which included representatives of agriculture, labor and welfare groups, has reported that the state has places now for 8,000. A similar commission has been appointed by Gov. Aandahl in North Dakota—a state in which the population has declined by 148,417 since 1940.

Such news gave them the faintest possibility of hope—and enough specific detail—that they could, at last, begin to realistically imagine alternate existences for themselves. They pulled atlases from the shelves of the camp libraries, made notes on elevation and climate, collected anecdotes from the camp's U.S.-raised United Nations staff. And from this jumble of amateur intelligence gathering, gossip and supposition, they built their own imagined realities of resettlement, revealed to themselves their desires and fears. Maybe today they were wind-chapped and numb, disarticulating the dimpled carcasses of pullets at a poultry processing plant in northern Michigan. Or, as when rumor spread of possible spots in California, maybe the next day, they were squinting against the sun, shedding burned skin like snakes, thinning the dates from medjool palms. Iowa is about the same elevation as Latvia, they noted, and from there it was an easy walk to the cornfields, the flat, shimmering heat, like a hand pressed against the backs of their necks, the itchy perfume of hot loam and manure.

For my grandparents, it made no difference which future version of themselves they allowed themselves to hope for, or hope against. No invitations came—from Iowa, or California, or Minnesota, or anywhere else.

Another year passed. And then another.

As more and more refugees left, there was no more need for so many classes at the Baltic University and my grandfather received a letter that his services were no longer needed as a lecturer.

Maruta returned from the hospital to finally live at home again, pale and weak, and distant. And then the seizures started. As she pitched and twisted, her head ratcheting on the floor of their room, my grandmother trying to hold her, to still her, pressing Maruta to her stomach, swollen now with her own fourth child, they could feel their worry pitch and ratchet with her: what had the neighbors heard, would they tell someone, thinking perhaps that to highlight anyone else's unfitness might raise their prospects of resettlement, should spots ever come up again?

And finally, the spots do come.

Under increasing pressure, the United States has agreed to admit 400,000 additional refugees for resettlement.

There are conditions, as outlined in official documents and debriefings by staff from the International Refugee Organization, which has been created by the United Nations to take over administration of the camps and their refugees:

To be eligible for consideration, each refugee requires a sponsor, someone stateside who will be willing to guarantee that there will be a place for the refugees to live, and that they will not take jobs from Americans. Once a sponsor is secured, the refugee must then submit to a twenty-two-step screening process, their files reviewed by the FBI, by the Counter Intelligence Corps of the U.S. Army, by the CIA, by the provost marshal general of the U.S. Army in Germany, as well as by special liaison investigators from British Intelligence. Their fingerprints will be checked against the fingerprint record center in Heidelberg, their names referenced against all the holdings of the Berlin Document Center, which houses all the Nazi files. They must sit for tests measuring physical, mental and occupational fitness.

But perhaps most critical of all: this opportunity will end in a little less than two years, on December 31, 1951. Refugees must complete all these steps within that time. Only those refugees whose applications are approved before the deadline will be eligible for this resettlement offer.

This is what the officials told them.

Here was what the refugees heard:

This is your last chance to leave.

Anything can derail an application: seizures, my grandparents note, trying to tamp down their fear. As can misbehaving children. An official complaint, no matter how small—whether for snatching an apple from one of the yards just beyond the camp, or breaking a window with a pebble cast out of boredom—could be enough, they have heard, to trigger a rejection on the grounds of moral turpitude.

To dream now was to dream only of your name pinned to the board announcing those who had reached the next stage: assignment to a refugee processing center.

This was the signal to pack whatever possessions you had

accumulated—the single suit, the woven scarf, your copies of *Who Is Who at the Baltic University* and *An Economic History of Europe Since 1750*—and prepare to move to new quarters, where you will be held just long enough for officials from the IRO to monitor whether any possible illnesses incubating inside you might surface before you are scheduled to step aboard the ships or planes bound for the States.

Sometimes, when their names finally appeared, those bound for the processing centers spent a giddy last night raising black market toasts to their good fortune—to Amerika!—only to blink into morning, and despite open eyes, receive nothing in return, whatever sight they possessed, and along with it, whatever chance they had at relocation—because the country that had sponsored them did not agree to sponsor a blind person—stolen by the schnapps made in those secret stills they had spent so many years deliberately not-seeing.

Finally, the letters V-e-r-z-e-m-n-i-e-k-s arranged themselves upon the board, and the family decamped for the regional processing center in Wentorf, assigned to block 16, room 112.

Once they reached the processing center, however, things stalled. First, pertussis: the children of block 16 wheezing and whooping their way through the next six months, one after another, pausing only to retch in enamel basins when it felt as if their lungs might rip and tear. Or was it measles: my grandmother running a brush through the baby's fever-matted hair, and there, on the scalp, a cheek, the soft side of a neck, the first inflamed splotches of red, freckling beneath the skin, then spreading.

Either way, they watched transport after transport leave without them as the baby recovered under quarantine.

And it is now, at this moment—as they remain suspended between final approval and infinite delay—the existing document trail skips. But this much remains certain: with just eight months before the deadline, after getting as close to the final stage of approval as one can get, short of stepping on the plane, they were dispatched back to their original DP camp, removed from the rosters of the processing center.

All that is left is to imagine into the void, to stitch supposition from the whisper-thin facts still threading through living memory.

Among the possible reasons they could have been sent back, their applications reset:

Perhaps, they had a different sponsor at this stage, one who ultimately backed out, who had hesitations suddenly about what would be required to take responsibility for a family of refugees.

Or perhaps, they themselves backed out, overwhelmed by doubts about where they were to be sent—Sentanobia, Mississippi?—and what they imagined they would have to do there, and so they asked for a new sponsor.

More likely:

My grandfather's military service had given someone, somewhere, one last cause for pause. Western military authorities had ruled that to have served in the Latvian Legion was not the same as to have served with the Nazi S.S. And this is what had released soldiers like my grandfather from the prison camp, and cleared his entry into the DP camp. The Nuremburg International Military Tribunal had been less clear. While the tribunal declared that the S.S. as a whole, including the Waffen S.S, the formation to which the legion had been assigned, was a criminal organization, it also did not say that this was automatic cause for a call-up on war-crimes charges. This was to be pursued and proven individually.

So ostensibly, if a person had been conscripted and had not committed any crimes, there was nothing to fear. But because there were legion members who had happily volunteered for service and who had engaged in war crimes—members of the infamous band of killers who rode the blue buses through Latvia's countryside helping to kill Jews, for example, had been absorbed into the earliest incarnation of the legion, and went on to fight only at the eastern front, just as the conscripts did—there remained confusion and unease about how to think of the legion.

There were rumors that applications from former legion members were being deliberately delayed. More than likely, the truth was somewhere between, as reviewers tried to make sense of what could not be reduced to a simple uncomplicated answer.

Ultimately, the U.S. Commission on Displaced Persons weighed in: all members of the legion should be considered to have been forcibly conscripted into service, and therefore, their service in it should not be grounds to deny their application.

And while it cleared the way for emigration, it also only further complicated things, forever lumping those who had most certainly committed war crimes with those who had not, so there would always be doubt about who was really who.

For three months, the family waited. My grandfather ticking and pacing, mumbling words to himself that only he could understand, rough, corrugated, the intonation implying a sentiment that fell somewhere between prayer and castigation.

And then finally, on July 5, with just five months to spare before the deadline to receive final approval, they were granted a spot in the processing center again, the chance to start the clearance phase again.

If they allowed themselves a new surge of hope, it was not much. Not more than a rap on the lintel could bear.

They had a sponsor now, and a possible destination, everything laid out in a letter my grandfather carried with him everywhere, so that he could not lose it, a letter signed by a representative of the Lutheran World Federation, informing him of the family's assigned place of residence once they had been cleared for passage to America: the Lutheran Hospice in Tacoma, Washington.

I know from the catalog of the family's possessions drawn up by the IRO that among my grandfather's books was an atlas. And as the day of their scheduled departure from Germany neared, they must have sought from it a tangible form of reassurance, that each time they flipped to the page that held the location of their future home, it was still there. They sought concrete facts. Soil conditions relative to Latvia. Average winter temperatures. Until they thought they knew where they were headed. But what of the things that cannot be quantified, geographies of experience and emotions that cannot be recorded or documented, only lived, and which form our most personal maps of home? That the air tasted of wood pulp and kelped water. That they would sleep beneath the edge of the sky where the pilots from the nearby air force base pushed their jets past the speed of sound—new planes for the older boy to admire.

And then Maruta had another seizure.

My grandmother was certain someone must have heard or seen something this time. Please, she silently willed their neighbors. Please don't tell anyone. Not when we're this close.

They knew their daughter needed to see a doctor, but they were also so fearful of being delayed again, of anything that could cause them to miss the final deadline for resettlement. They told themselves they had a better chance of getting Maruta the help she needed in America, if only they could get there.

And so, although it roused in them a deep distress, they agreed that they would spend the remaining hours in the camp pretending that nothing had happened, lying if necessary, and hiding Maruta from any possible scrutiny.

She waited as long as she could to bring Maruta into the medical screening room for the family's final preflight evaluation.

Any recent changes in her condition? the doctor asked.

No, my grandmother said, and stared hard at Maruta, as if with only her eyes she could fix her to the floor, will her limbs to stay limp. She heard only the pounding of her own heart, a tripping rhythm. Then, the scratching of doctor's pen: *Approved for emigration.*

THEY CARRIED three suitcases and one rucksack between them, the contents meticulously logged: one petticoat, five handkerchiefs, three spoons, two cups, one knife, one men's suit, three plates, one nightdress, two children's training pants, one apron, one hammer, one camera, two undershorts, three blankets, one bedsheet, one pair of child's overalls, one boy's coat, one scarf.

There are no toys listed, on the manifest, no jewelry and only one book—an English dictionary.

This is what they would use to start their new life.

Even as they settled into their seats, their names and refugee numbers pinned to their chests, Livija watched Maruta closely, fearing that another seizure could come at any moment, and they would be ordered off the plane.

It was only when she felt the plane's nose catch and rise that she let herself believe that this was truly happening, that they were leaving.

What my father remembers:

Not his mother's humming fear, but that their plane was a Lockheed Constellation, the first plane he had ever seen close up, the fuselage sleek and silver, a mirror in which he could see himself.

That the stewardess took him to meet the pilots in the cockpit.

That they touched down in Greenland to refuel the plane, and it was night, but he could not sleep and when he looked out the window, he saw the world as pinpricks of light.

He remembers New York, their port of entry, the smells of Penn Station, tar pitch, creosote, heated steel, pigeon dander.

He remembers their first apartment in downtown Tacoma, not far from the train station where they disembarked, the cascading brick of it, the steep creep of the stairs, the way the windows let in the honking wail of the tugs shouldering through Commencement Bay just across the street, the sea-scratched voices of the longshoremen commuting to work by rowboat.

In my grandfather's billfold: a letter of recommendation from the former president of the Baltic University, the deepening creases an indication of how often he must have removed it and read it, trying to reacquaint himself with who he had been once, however briefly:

> I was always impressed by his ability and high qualification in the field of scientifics and teaching work, by his assiduity, and his present and friendly character in the relations with the members of the teaching staff. . . .

As it turned out, he had no cause to bring it out for anyone else.

Instead, in America, the former chair of economic theory with one eye was qualified to mop floors and wax linoleum, to pour molten metal into molds at the local foundry, to spread roofs with tar and to lay asphalt shingles. My grandmother, the former accountant for Latvia's leading bacon export factory, took on piecework, sewing at home.

And when they could, together, with the children, whenever they weren't in school, they picked fruit from the local truck farms spread along the Puyallup Valley, in the shadow of Mt. Rainier, urging little hands to gather flats of raspberries and strawberries, to lop the stems of daffodils bound for elaborate bouquets.

They saved. Stubs of pencils, scraped sharp with the edges of knives. Seeds collected from empty roadsides. Thread. Pennies. They spoke of the present, using the old tongue, kept the construction of their sentences from reaching too far into the past.

But the past has a way of resisting silence, of asserting itself on the present without ever requiring a word.

I think of my father, the boy who watched war planes, who slept in the Luftwaffe barracks, who grew up to become an aerospace engineer, an expert in the composition of materials required to build planes and helicopters and shuttles and missiles, in particular glass.

He would devote years to developing a way to take this most brittle of materials to the very edge of breaking, yet remain strong enough to withstand the crushing forces of reentry.

XVII

In the last year, my leg has healed so that only a small scar remains from the dog's bite, the size and color of a currant, like those a starling is busily beaking from the bushes at the edge of Ausma's yard.

Just look at the state of my garden, she says, as we break from our embrace. Do you even recognize it? Most days, my hip hurts so much, I can't do very much. I have to keep stopping to rest. My souvenir from Siberia, all these pains in my body.

Harijs emerges from the barn, trailing wisps of hay.

You! he says, as I kiss his cheek. All the way from America! Tell me, how long did it take you to get here? Did you fly here, through the sky, or did you come by boat?

You can't be serious, Ausma says. She came by airplane! It would take weeks if she went by sea!

Tell me, do you have the same trees in America?

Ausma shakes her head. You can't really expect her to answer that—it's different, of course, and the same.

What about wolves—do you have wolves in America?

That's enough with your silly questions, Ausma says. Next thing, you'll be telling her about all the times you nearly died. I'm sure she's tired. Let's make tea.

———

AUSMA HAS placed a vase of mock orange next to my bed and laid at my feet a linen blanket made on my great-grandmother's loom. But sleep refuses to come.

I listen to the cows cudding grass outside my window. Then the cats spitting and fighting somewhere beyond the cows, biting one another's backs, releasing puffs of fur for the chickens to bob over come morning. Then: the sound of something howling, a piercing monotone hymn that lasts for what feels like hours.

How did you sleep? Asuma asks the next morning, placing a cup of tea on the table in front of me. The radio sings to us a list of reasons that Latvian women are the best in the world.

Did you hear the dogs howling? I ask.

Dogs? says Ausma. I didn't hear any dogs.

A FEW DAYS LATER, in the archives of the local museum, I find a stack of transcripts from interviews conducted with survivors of the same mass exile that included Ausma. They appear to be part of a school project, village children assigned to record the memories of local deportees.

Each interview includes a questionnaire.

Did you know anyone who died?

Yes, a man circles.

Who?

My father.

How did the person die? Choose one.

Suicide, he circles.

One woman, when invited to describe what life was like for her in Siberia, says only this:

We lived under pine trees, and once, a wolf bit me.

MY COUSIN—she of the exaltation of cows—has taken a job for the summer as a rural mail carrier. She has just graduated university with a degree in economics, but she is not sure she wants to leave the countryside, even though there is no call here for the theories of marketing she spent all those years memorizing. A relative in England has invited her to come stay with her, to see what jobs she might find there. But she is hesitant.

In a city, she says, can you ever be alone, the way you're alone here, with only quiet? Where do you go to remind yourself you and your problems are small? I don't think I want to get too far from that feeling. I want to be able to go walking in the fields by myself, looking for wild caraway, and never see another soul, except maybe my cows.

So for now she drives her mail truck over roads built from nothing more than what is there, impacted topsoil and muck, and she hopes maybe her stuttering tires might jar a decision loose inside her.

The box of mail on the seat next to her reveals the existence of a nowhere that even she—who has lived in this countryside her whole life, who celebrates its remoteness, its secret caraway fields and cow-quiet—had no idea existed. These are not houses, she thinks. They are burrows. Or dens. Holes above ground, through which it is possible to slip from the surface of this life into a forgotten one, where spluttering candles provide the only light; where bed is a greasy blanket on the floor;

where what at first seems a carpet is in fact a thick layer of fleas. Gradually, from the dim, other occupants materialize: old men and old women, or not yet old men and women made old by work or by drink, it is so difficult to tell, their faces as haggard and featureless as a turnip at the bottom of a crate that has been left too long in one of the subterranean root cellars that are a feature of every country home.

They ask her to open and read aloud the letters that come in their names, and whether this is because their eyes are no good, or they have never learned to make sense of the marks on the page, she doesn't ask. Sometimes, they implore her to take their signed government checks, their pensions back to the village to cash, and she can bring the money the next time she comes with the mail. And maybe these groceries, too? Can you write it down if I tell you?

One day, I accompany my cousin on her route. There are miles of brooding woods, roads so dusty she must at times turn on her wipers to see.

We visit solemn, stout apartment blocks, Googie-gilled and cold-eyed as carp, like the blocks of developments you see in the capital, mile upon mile of Stalinist-era architecture, stretched along promenades wide enough to accommodate several lanes of Zaparozhets cars, some of the last visible reminders of the Communist years. Specifically: the promise of cheap, fair, practical housing for everyone.

They are also reminders of the unanticipated consequences of exile. One day, it occurred to Soviet officials that between all those killed or wounded in the war, and all those who fled, and all those they had already banished to Siberia, they would never be able to find the kind of replacement labor required to run the country's new collective farms in Latvia alone. So they reached across the republics, gathered up workers and scattered them throughout the countryside. And they raised hundreds of these developments to house them. The problem was that many of these workers had never farmed before, nor did they find the idea particularly enjoyable. To them the landscape was not bucolic. It was grim, bewildering, backward-looking. They were city dwellers, marooned between fields of sugar beets and goat-trampled bracken.

At a distance, it's easy to feel a kind of smug disdain for these Soviet-era apartments that remain. But up close, following my cousin as she drops women's magazines through mail slots, hand-delivers a government check to a woman who half-hides behind her front door, as the television in the background sings the theme of a Russian game show, they strike me as strangely beautiful, the way all attempts at a carefully calculated uniformity are quietly interrupted by the fragile, yet persistent business of everyday life: the balconies flagged with laundry-line semaphores that wink *fuchsia, chevron, Spice Girls, tropical paradise, black lace*; the naughty graffiti in English written in too much haste and left to drool down the pebble-dash walls, a preteen laughing too hard at his own sad-silly dirty joke—"Poop/fuck"; the potted sweet peas that throw legs over railings; the cardboard boxes left turned on their sides in the bushes with pillows stuffed inside—thrones upon which the stray cats can perch like queens and tooth their chicken bones or preen their sable coats; the old woman in sandals and knee-socks who brooms with twigs the surrounding dirt footpaths in patterns that resemble clouded skies.

From here, the mail route takes us past crumbing radio towers, down hoof-trampled paths that reveal at their end clearings, but no evidence of the hooves that tramped the way here, or the house and barns which must shelter them, just a crude box on a post, and manged dogs with screaming pink skin that spring from the weeds, like highway bandits, to mouth the truck's wheels, until my cousin throws food out the driver's side window to distract them long enough so that she can reverse.

The route also takes us past the old family farm, where we park the truck and wade into the weeds so that I can monitor the continued and uninterrupted progress of its unmaking.

It's now been five years since my first visit, and the floor has begun buckling upward, toward the sky, then folding back upon itself like rock from some great prehistoric rift. The roof that remains bows so low in places that it almost, but does not quite touch the ruptured seams of the floor.

Do you think it's possible houses have something that's equivalent to a soul? my cousin asks. Something that's left in the house when someone is born there, or someone dies there?

I don't want to ruin her question with an answer. So instead I try to list all our ancestors who were born and who died at Lembi.

And they were the last, she says.

SHE WORKS the truck down a narrow road made from earth that threads through forest so stolid and imposing and end-lessly repeating that I imagine for a moment that we must be driving in circles.

The soil beneath the trees is undisturbed, soft with the memories of centuries of rotted things. The light that filters through the branches is silvered like lichen, and feels as if it's never before been taken into human lungs. I imagine these are the kind of woods where the werewolf Thies might have hidden postbanishment.

Under the truck's wheels, the road spits dust like a string of letters appearing on a blank page. Otherwise, nothing stirs.

After ten minutes of driving, we come to a stop next to a makeshift mailbox nailed to a hemlock that nods its branches at our approach.

My cousin explains that there is a very old woman who lives all alone in a hut hidden in this forest, built only from what it has given her. Once a week, she hikes several kilometers to this box to check for word from the world beyond hers.

No one knows the reason for her self-imposed exile, just that something happened that made her choose the company of pines over people, the language of birds and stones and water over human speech.

> Other people are related to other people
> Me, poor me, I am kin only to trees:
> Ash, maple, oak
> They are my blood, they love me like family

The old stories hold that the forest is a place out of time, where the normal rules of language and comprehension and knowledge do not apply, where miracles are possible. Not miracles in the religious sense, but holy in their own way, like the no-weight of a vole's skeleton, the murmuring of old leaves that twist in the wind like withered tongues.

And maybe this is why I find myself debating whether I should ask my cousin to let me out here, so that I can go and find this woman who must have been alive in the war, who is old enough to know what it is to feel pain, and be the source of another's pain.

But even if I could follow the smell of bramble fire to her open door and a crow-eyed welcome, an old head bobbing, I already know that the question I most want to ask her, this woman who has so deliberately lost herself in these woods which I cannot see my way through, is also my only answer, an instruction, a command, a plea: how to live with this hurt.

XVIII

W AS YOUR life in Siberia all sadness?
   Not at all. People laughed. There were dances.
Did you feel joy?
Now, I wouldn't go that far.

IF IT WAS POSSIBLE to be grateful for a job to which you are
sentenced, Ausma was grateful for the herding assignment: a
mob of ewes, 350 solid solemn things, spotted, their hindquar-
ters like two heavy half-moons. A new breed for Siberia, she had
heard, brought from one of the more mountainous republics in
the west, on the assumption they would introduce, with their
tough, scrubby bloodlines, a disposition toward hardiness.

Her job was to trail them into the fields, so they could
nose away the snow in search of fresh growth. They had
been locked away for the worst of the winter and were eager
to graze, grunting happily to themselves. She watched them
eat, wriggling and pink, recently skinned of their long heavy
coats. At least the job was familiar, one of the first chores given
to a child in the Latvian countryside, dispatched to the fields
almost as soon she can walk with a lunch pail in her hand
and the latest generation in a long line of soft-mouthed farm

dogs—jaws like a farrier's nippers, pinching but never puncturing flesh—trotting behind. There were no fences, not then,
not now, not ever, and so it was up to child and dog to keep
the animals from following some unnamable bovine instinct
into the underbrush or bogs. The quickest children learned to
use the landscape to pen the animals, to drive them lowing to
a V in the river, so that the waters can mind them on three
sides. Then all that is left for you is to make a bed in the grass
behind them, stitching colored mittens or making whistles
from the grass.

Ausma had just started to settle in when she saw one sheep
drop. Followed by another and another, until the whole herd
was keeling. They would not rise, no matter how hard she
tugged. Slowly, it became clear to her that the collective had
shorn their coats according to the schedule they had always
followed with the sheep who had already lived in this region
for a long time. But this new breed was not accustomed to the
scalding cold that still lingered as winter turned toward spring.
Now, they were too numb-legged to hobble the kilometer back
to the barn on their own.

She would have no choice but to carry them back herself,
one at a time. Then maybe she could take them to the back in
the barn, cover them with her body, rub their legs between her
chapped and cracking palms.

She heaved the first sheep over her shoulders and began her
staggered walk.

After the first hour, she could no longer feel her arms. After
the second hour, she bawled along with the ewes.

The snowmelt could not come fast enough, and even if it
brought mud and mosquitoes, at least it meant the sheep could
carry themselves home again, and she could follow their heavy

hoofed gait through the slop, looking for what the cold had concealed.

Bird cherry. Buttercup. Currant. Peony. Violet.

Then: could it really be winter again so quickly?

Out into the snow one more—there is no escape from it—this time to the forests, a slice of bread in her coat pocket for lunch; within minutes it would be frozen. Sometimes, if hunger's nattering reached a particularly incessant pitch, she learned to snap off small pieces and then set them on her tongue to melt as she sawed. Otherwise, she would save it for the fire set later in the old metal barrel, where workers were allowed to come and stand for a few moments and unthaw their hands, release the shape of the saw's grip. There she would hold the bread over the fire until her fingers whinged and smoked.

Those laboring alongside her were mostly women. All the men had been killed in the war or surrendered too many limbs to field surgeons' saws to manage the most demanding assignments, like forestry duty. Mornings, before sunrise, she and the other women stomped deep into the taiga, where they were expected to spend the next ten hours felling pines or birch, then stacking the wood. Ausma could barely lift the axe they gave her; hungry, weak, she quickly fell behind. No work, no grain, the brigade captain scolded.

What would it be like to lie down and never get up again, to rest like the body at the edge of the rail tracks, slowly shedding all ties to the living. To let leaves fall, covering your eyes. Frost rime your skin. Surrendering to the thicket all traces of who you are and where you are from.

She had given up all hope of her own life to come here and care for her brother and mother, as she had done back at the farm. She had imagined, if she could endure that, this could not ask her to do anything harder than what she had already done. But already, this quickly, it was beyond her. And now, in her failure, she was certain she had sentenced the three of them to their deaths.

Oh, sister, her brother said, when she came home, unable to lift her arms higher than her waist. Don't cry.

I can't go back there, she said. But if I don't, we're all lost.

No, we're not, he said. You can do this.

You make it sound so simple, she said.

It is, he said. You just need the right axe.

He might not be able to handle hard labor, but sensing that survival in the settlements was not just about what your body could endure, but also about forging connections, he had asked for a job that suited a one-legged man, and had been assigned to watch the horse barns at night. In this way he had made friends with the blacksmith.

I'll take care of it, he said.

And he did, bringing her a modified axe that was lighter, easier to handle.

She kept up with the others after that, swung as cleanly as if splitting head from neck. She taught her body how to remain in one place, while her mind drifted to another.

Those on forest duty often worked in two-week shifts, and sometimes, at night, as the trees led them farther into the taiga, they boarded in abandoned settlements near its edges. The houses where they stayed were so empty their voices echoed.

Usually there was a stove, and someone who offered to stay awake in order to keep stoking it, but it was impossible for any of them to hold their eyes open long. It was too cold to wash, too cold to undress. After a few days, the smell warned them even before they could register the dancing at their jackets' seams and along their collars—a building stench like leaves left in gutters to rot. When she finally came home at the end of her rotation, her mother would not let her through the door.

Not with all your friends, too, Alma said.

So Ausma stripped everything off in the yard, cold pricking her exposed skin like the touch of nettles' leaves. She dropped her skirt and coat into a metal pail that her mother filled with water. Finally, they boiled everything for several hours on the makeshift stove they built outside from bricks of river mud, until tiny fawn-colored specks scummed the surface.

What they ate:

Slices of cold-blackened potatoes.

Tiny translucent fish, no more than a swallow, collected from the creek, using sheets as nets.

Nuts husked from the cones of the Siberian cedars, to be savored under the tongue like hard candy, smoky and resinous, like tasting the dregs of an old fire. Birch seeds, catkins.

They boiled grass and the leaves of black currants and drank it like tea.

In the early days, when they still lived with the Russian exile, the one who was sorry this had happened to them, she would set aside a shot of milk for Ausma, thin and green, but still, an extra portion. To help you saw faster, she said.

And when Ausma slopped scalding water over her foot, and had to miss several days' work, the woman brought a bowl to her bed.

What is it? Ausma asked.

Something special, the woman said. To help you heal faster.

Potatoes, Ausma saw. Laced with cream. Not the usual thin filings of frozen milk, scraped from the top of the pails they kept out in the cold. Real cream. Thick like sap, pleasingly sour, like the first bite of a cherry. For years, Ausma would remember it as the best meal she had ever eaten.

THOSE WHO were sent to the settlements across the river and never came back—there were stories that toward the end they ate nettles, scraped the skin from birch trees with their teeth as if stripping meat from bones. And maybe it's true they held rocks in their mouths, worrying them with their tongues. But did they really dig the ticks from their arms with their nails, snap their teeth at the circling midges, like dogs?

Nothing is impossible when nothing is possible.

Ausma knows this now.

But it is easier to believe that maybe, first, they ate the lice.

WHAT THEY wore:

Whatever they had time to pack.

Most of them had no time to pack.

In the earliest weeks, they wore whatever they were wearing when the soldiers came for them. Sometimes, the soldiers took pity on those who were too stunned to assemble a case and dumped the contents of drawers onto sheets, then pressed the bundles into reluctant hands. This is what they did for Ausma's mother. She had stood, rooted, unmoving, because she imagined they would soon shoot her, so what was the point of doing anything at all.

One woman was said to have made her Siberian debut in a suit and heels. There are stories of children who came barefoot, in nightdresses.

Where once she dreamed of a jacket trimmed with a bit

of fur, a hat with one winging feather like Livija wore when Ausma went to visit her in Riga, new items of desire emerge:

Telogreika jackets, turgid, ponderous things, unsentimental, gray as rat fur or green as spoiled meat, first tested by Red Army soldiers dug into the trenches around a starving Stalingrad, or gunning trucks across Lake Ladoga's icy expanse, trying to outrace German bombers. Now the uniform of the stout aunties with their giant heaving bosoms cursing tractors through the Siberian muck.

Valenki boots, long the footwear of Russia's unfortunates, and also a synonym for suffering, stupidity. *Dumb as a valenki*, the Russians said when they harbored particular vitriol for someone. For the exiles, valenkis meant their only defense against the creeping black of frostbite. They were made from nothing more than felt, wool, oily with lanolin, boiled and rolled into the shape of galoshes by hands red and blistered from the sulfuric acid dips that make the fibers shrink and mat. The boots were cumbersome, quick to suck up moisture, so that it seemed as if you are walking with whole sheep strapped to your feet.

You could tell a valenki wearer from a distance simply by her gait: slow, sluggish, heavy-soled. When the wet boots dried, they shrank to the shape of the wearer's foot. Like hinges rusted shut, they could not be budged. If you worked in valenkis, you would likely sleep in valenkis. More than a few were buried in valenkis.

LATE SUMMER, the time of harvest. She swung from the cab of a moving combine, intending to drop at a run, so that she could move to the next lane of mown hay. Instead, she landed on her back. She felt something slip, the pop of gristle. She didn't tell anyone, simply removed the kerchief from her head and used it to bind her ribs and her back, to try to hold in the pain. No work, she told herself, no rations. But as she tried to fork the hay into piles, she felt her vision dip and flutter, then shrink to a pinprick. She wasn't conscious when they brought her home in the back of one of the hay wagons.

Her brother found her, curled on her side in the corner of the kitchen where they lived.

If I told you you could have four hands and three legs, could you get up? he said. I can't go very fast, but between us, until you heal, we can be almost one person.

So she grew four hands and three legs, though it hurt.

It hurt her to watch her brother struggling with the rake, his crutch slipping. It hurt her to watch him pitch and tumble.

She couldn't decide if watching this hurt as much as the pain in her back, but she also knew she needed to make quota, so that they could eat, so she just let the hurts accumulate, like the piles of wild ryegrass and clover slowly rising in front of them, becoming something thick, repetitive, never-ending. Rick of hay, rick of hay.

TIME UNRAVELED, like the strands of the blanket that Ausma had thought to bring from what remained in the farmhouse.

Thread by thread, gray, green, yellow, brown, her mother unloosened the weave, then summoned from the new-old skeins sets of mittens.

Her needles coaxed patterns from memory, calling on what her mother had taught her, as her mother had taught her before that, the ancient symbols, a ledger of fates:

Moon. Morning star. Sun. Sun, who, it is said, among other things, keeps special watch over the unlucky.

They were still not allowed to leave the settlement. But a neighbor, who had received permission to travel to the market in Moscow to sell her own wares, offered to take the mittens and bring back whatever money they might make. Whether it was the help of the Sun, or the intricacy of Alma's handwork, all the mittens sold, and the friend returned with money, enough money that they were able to negotiate the purchase of a piglet from one of their fellow kolkholzniks.

Really, it was not a pig they were buying, but the chance to believe they might have a life that was, as Ausma's mother put it, *half-human.*

And yet it was a pig they bought, in the end.

Just not a sow.

Sows were acceptable for private use; hogs summoned a tax.

So it was not a pig they bought, but a penalty.

Two thousand rubles. Due now.

No more blanket to unravel, no more mittens to bring to market. Nothing left to trade to pay the fine.

How do you live less than half a life?

Will potato peelings buried deep enough eventually sprout? What does it mean when you open your mouth to speak and your words smell of bitter pith, fruit turning?

A letter, slipped in Alma's hands, helped them change the answers they might have given.

I am writing to tell you that you are still owed money for milk that you delivered to the dairy cooperative in Gulbene before you had to go away. . . . I am sorry that it has taken me so

long to find your new address. I have enclosed the amount
you are due and will make a note in my ledger.

And now, one more entry for the ledger of fates:
Cow.

Even after they had settled the fine for owning the hog,
they still had enough left over from what the head of the dairy
back in their hometown had sent them to purchase their own
heifer. Only one hundred rubles, because she was old and her
teats were shriveled. But they spoke to her, told her how much
she meant to them, sang her songs about sun and green fields.
They named her Gauja, after one of the major rivers running
through their region of Latvia. They fed her cedar nuts and
shoots of grass they collected by hand, spooned her currant-leaf
tea. Soon, she was singing, too, the milk from her teats sound-
ing each morning in the tin that once held the old farm's honey.
Then they would pour the milk into bowls, and set the bowls
outside to freeze. Then they would tip the frozen bowls into
pillowcases, releasing the bricks of milk.

By then, they had received permission to travel as far as
Tomsk, on day passes. And so, once they had set aside a little milk for themselves, Ausma began to haul the pillowcases
to market. First, she registered with the settlement's security
office. Then, she walked to the nearest rail line, about five kilometers away. Sometimes she could catch a ride on one of the
collective wagons, oxen already plodding that way. She had no
money to buy a ticket, so when she found a departing train,
she latched herself to its side. She rode this way for the thirty-
kilometer journey to Tomsk, like a tick, her cheeks reddening,
then blackening in the battering wind.

———

AFTER COW:

Then came little house.

Long abandoned, it sat at the edge of the river where they hunted the waters with their makeshift nets. Their Russian friend, the exile who had let them sleep in a corner in her kitchen, had told them about it. Now that you are making a little money, you should find a place of your own, she said. No one will mind if you use this old house, so long as you make all the repairs.

They redaubed the walls with mud gathered from the creek bed.

It didn't take long with only one room.

Ausma and her mother shared the only bed; her brother made a nest of blankets on the floor, near the stove.

Collectively, the exiles were like fish trapped beneath the ice of the river in winter, suspended in this new half-life, caught between. They did not want to be here, but they were here. So what could they do but collect the seeds of wild geranium and cosmos from the woods and meadows, then plant them in window boxes, scatter them behind the outdoor stove so that at least while they cook they can see something beautiful. They played at picnics, putting blankets down beneath birch trees that looked so much like the ones they once knew. They said, Here, this is saffron bread, and everyone chewed the hard loaf made with flour doctored from the sawdust of birch bark or crushed dried clover, and laughed and pantomimed delight.

They bined wild hops, brewed beer, fermented foraged

fruits. Boys, looped, took a bicycle from the collective equipment area, and nested it in the crook of a tree. It made no sense, which was exactly why it seemed so brilliant at the time. Dangling from the branches, they toasted first everything—To bicycles!—then everyone they could think of.

To Ausma!

She ignored the boys who shrilled at her, like birds. Kept her distance. She didn't have time for that. She barely had time to sleep.

What she did for distraction:

Sometimes, at night, if she was not too exhausted, Ausma would practice embroidering scraps of fabric in the style her Russian friend had taught her: elaborate still lifes of tulips and lilacs; a composition of meadow clover, which, when viewed closely, rewarded the attentive with a secret single stem of four leaves.

Occasionally, she tried to read. When they were finally allowed to receive packages from home, her godmother sent her a novel, a sprawling retelling of the history of Riga. Still, there were nights when she could only bring herself to read a single word before she would shut the covers, unsure of how long she would need to make these pages last, if this was the only book she would ever have again.

Other exiles drew heated nails down scraps of larch to serve as headstones. They coaxed chess sets from bone, called instruments from shoe leather and strands of their own hair. They picked apart bandages to crochet shawls and decorative collars that lay on their shoulders, spotted with red.

For some, bark doubled as paper, unwound from the birch trunks with callused hands. On scraps the size of postcards, they nubbed messages to relatives in Latvia, never forgetting the censors' eyes.

They wrote: *Warm summer wishes!*

They wrote: *Remember your friends in faraway Siberia.*

ONE NIGHT, Ausma went to see a movie in the collective's community center. Here, they listened to poetry celebrating the proletariat, attended award ceremonies and medal presentations for those who exceeded their work quotas and so honored the state. Fastest Milker. Best Reaper. Honored Stacker of Wood. Some nights there were dances, work-battered bodies spinning through limping waltzes, the happy heat and stink of limbs given over to effort that no one else can claim. Other nights: old movies, screened for the appropriate narratives of individual sacrifice and collective redemption.

Dumb with fatigue, Ausma sat in the back with Stalin's portrait, her legs numbing on a folding chair, and she stared at the images flickering on the wall in front of her.

She did not know how long she had been watching before it occurred to her that this was in fact a Latvian film, set in Latvia, and all the actors were speaking in Latvian.

Rather than stir something inside her, this realization saddened her.

How much did that old life really ever matter if she could forget it so quickly?

And then, one March, the month of their taking, now four years on, as the ice began to release its grip and the rivers and streams began to tremble, a sound so loud as to be mistaken for the vibration of train wheels rushing along tracks, it so happened, that at the same time, nearly four thousand kilometers away, in Moscow, the man who had engineered their taking, and so many other takings, all those trains in motion, fell to his bedroom floor, next to a copy of *Pravda* and his pocket watch.

A blood vessel in his head burst, then pooled.

When help finally arrived, it was too late to undo the damage. It is difficult to find a capable doctor when you have already banished so many.

Across Siberia, the exiles were gathered in party halls and community centers, as the news from Moscow spread:

Stalin is dead.

There were aunties who wailed and smashed their chests against the glass of the community center portraits, their breasts level with his mustache. But later, after those aunties left, there were others who flipped the portrait over so they did not have to look at that mustache again.

With the death of the architect of their exile, the banished began to compose letters, like this one penned by my great-grandmother in 1952, asking to exist again:

> *Please, your Honorable Minister. My family and I were exiled to Siberia in 1949. There are only three of us here: myself, my son and my daughter. I am old and ill, and can no longer work. My son tries to work, but he is an invalid, missing his left leg. We have never been members of a seditious group. My dearest wish is to be able to return to my home to sleep at last in the sandy soil that also holds my ancestors. I beg your permission to do this.*

I FIND this letter in a file in an unmarked warehouse located at the end of an unpaved service road in Riga, hidden behind the bulk of an old factory where fifteen thousand workers—the same number of people sent to Siberia in the first mass exile, in 1941—once assembled Soviet transistor radios and record players the size of kitchen tables. Now the factory building is shuttered, for rent. The brokers kindly refer to it in promotional literature as a fine example of brutalist architecture.

Anyone searching for the records of those who disappeared in the days of Siberia will be told that they must first find the factory; only then will they find the warehouse that now holds all the files from that time, the secret orders, all those handwritten letters addressed to *Dear Honorable Ministers*, like the one signed by my great-grandmother Alma.

Once, when I asked Ausma if she knew why they were sent away, the reason for all that they had suffered, she answered immediately: *The bees.*

After the war, when the process of collectivization began, and property lines were being redrawn, possessions divided, a man who lived not far from Lembi, someone suddenly of some authority in the Party, initiated his own plan to redistribute local wealth and personally requested the delivery of Lembi's hives to his own farm.

To which my great-grandfather was said to reply: Not even when I am dead.

Four years after his fall from the loft, his widow and his son and his daughter were on a train to Siberia under secret order.

And all the hives from Lembi were spotted on the Party official's land.

In the family's declassified file in Riga, there is no mention of the bees.

Only a document signed by officials from Stalin's Ministry

for State Security that appears in the file of anyone who was ever sent to Siberia as a special exile.

It says:

STRICTLY SECRET

And:

DESIGNATED FOR EXILE

And:

EVIDENCE: _____

(*Choose one: bandit, nationalist, kulak*)

Kulak was the most popular choice, filling in the blank 29,030 times. It means wealthy peasant, as in: *The kulak possesses 33 hectares of land, 2 horses, 19 cows, 12 pigs and 3 paid laborers.*

This was the reason selected for my family. That they were peasants—who owned too much land.

In the end, one could say that the farm that my great-great-grandfather struggled to buy so the family could remain connected to the land of their ancestors became the very reason they would ultimately be exiled from it.

And how thin the line that distinguishes one wealthy peasant from another, those who were deemed threatening enough to be taken from those who were deemed safe enough to leave.

Only three hectares, in my family's case—the equivalent of seven and a half acres.

Or, by another accounting:

One brood of hens.

On that day, years ago, when my great-grandmother demanded that her husband evict his cousin and the cousin's wife, and the wife's marauding chickens, from Lembi, that meant buying up the cousin's share of land in order to get him to leave. The cousin's holding and my great-grandfather's existing holdings added up to thirty-three hectares.

And a kulak becomes a kulak for every hectare over thirty.

As for my great-grandmother's plea, the files indicate it was not answered until 1956. When a response was finally issued, it came by form letter, curt, bureaucratic, unemotional:

You may return to your original place of residence.

They sold everything they had accumulated—Gauja, the crude furniture they had built, the bed. They used the profits to buy train tickets. A free ride here, said Ausma. Now we pay our own way home.

Ausma kept a little money back to buy a bolt of fabric to take to a woman in the settlement, someone too old and crippled to work for the collective but who supported herself by taking on small sewing jobs. She asked the woman to make her a dress. To make up for the one that she had been measured for by the seamstress back in Gulbene, all those years ago, on the day everyone was taken, and which she had never collected. She always wondered what had happened to that dress, which her mother had hoped would save her.

THEIR FIRST train journey had taken three weeks. This time, they reached the Latvian border in just fourteen days. Ausma and her mother and brother disembarked at the same station from which they left eight years before, not far from the cemetery where my great-grandmother wrote of her longing to be buried. She would get her wish, dying three years after the family's return from Siberia.

But she never did return to her original place of residence.

By then, Lembi had been absorbed into one of the local collective farms, sections of the house converted to stalls, people living in the barns.

Sometimes, it seems any answer you choose can explain everything and nothing.

EVIDENCE: _____

Choose one:

And someone writes *bees.*

And someone else writes *hens.*

And someone else writes *kulak.*

But there is another possibility, one that I suspect my grandmother must have known. In addition to owning farm-land, the exiled often had connections to someone who fled the country and did not come back. Or, worse still, to someone who'd fought for the German side.

If you had asked my grandmother, Who is responsible for the loss of the farm called Lembi and the subsequent exile of everyone who lived upon it, would she have written *Me?*

XIX

SHE TRIED to send them a message to let them know that she had survived, but it never reached them.

They tried to send her a message to let her know that they had almost not survived, but it never reached her.

For a long time, they were upset with her, because they thought maybe her silence was a choice, that she did not want to remember them.

And then they would worry that her silence actually meant she was dead.

And then she would worry that their silence actually meant they were dead.

In this way, they spent more than ten years, trapped in silence and paranoia and misunderstanding.

It wasn't until she had safely reached the States, and they had safely returned from Siberia, that they were able to find each other again, through letters.

Dearest Sister, We are overjoyed to know that you are alive. When so much time passed with no word from you, we decided we should give up ever hearing from you again. Gradually, our hurt and our anger subsided and we wanted

*to try once more to find out what had happened to you, but
we didn't know where to start. We were so grateful to get
this letter. We realize now that you tried to reach us, too,
and that you also had no idea where we were, or what had
happened to us.*

As much as these letters offered the family a temporary stay
against the realities of exile, they also had a strange way of
simultaneously magnifying its effects. The family quickly
learned to read for what was not there, to be sensitive to that
which was avoided. The letters taught them to think in terms of
how much they could leave unsaid while still appearing to say
something. They told stories not about what really happened,
but stories designed to help you guess what really happened
when what really happened was impossible to say—a truthful
misdirection, a necessary fiction, cribbed entirely from fact.

*You may not know, but after the war, I spent some time
working in a coal mine, and one day, the mine collapsed
and my left leg was crushed. I developed gangrene and the
bone became tubercular and so it was amputated to my hip.
Ausma is now the strongest one in the family and our sole
breadwinner. Not long after I recovered from my accident,
we went far away to work for a time. Just when our mother
began to think she would like to pay a visit to her husband's
grave, and to the graves of her parents, we were given
permission to return here, to Gulbene. We have a new place
to live now. We depend on the kindness of relatives who are
letting us stay with them. Ausma is working for the local
kolkhoz, tending chickens.*

It was as if they were squinting through keyholes at one another, seeing only cropped or partial glimpses of their lives.

Or maybe they were more like people trying to force the shape of constellations from individual stars. They assumed relationships, presumed significance where maybe there was none.

Or was it more like divination, like throwing bones, studying the patterns of the fragments that emerged, as if this could finally answer the real questions that they had for each other, but could never voice: Was I right to flee? Do you ever wish you'd never left? Are things really so terrible where you are? Are they really so wonderful where you are? Are you scared? Are you happy? Which of us is truly the fortunate one—the one who was taken, or the one who was left?

Hello, Amerika!
Dear family, far away!
Loving wishes from the Motherland!
My most precious child!

Here is some news about the cows: we just bought a heifer,
and she is a such a soft milker, with pliable teats!

Thank you for the coffee, the candy, the peanut butter, the
cooking oil, the raisins, the perfumes and the medicine for the
children.

We are cutting wood now.
We are waiting for snow.
We are putting up a greenhouse.
There has been no rain, everything is dry.

There has been too much rain.
This is a good hay year.
There are so many tomatoes.
There are no nuts to gather.

Today I went mushrooming and found more than twenty!
Bilberries, too!

The barley is so beautiful this year.

Thank you for the money; I used it to buy a coat to replace
the one I had that was twenty years old.

Thank you for the money, we have been doing without
refrigeration for the last two years, and our old TV showed
only pictures of fog.

Thank you so much for your help with the car. I found a 1984
Ford Escort, violet in color. I used to be scared to even dream
of a car that didn't fill with clouds of dust and that in cold
weather I could drive without shaking. Now that dream has
been realized! I am still having a little trouble learning how to
drive it. A Ford is no Zaparozhets!

Pork is selling at a good price.

We harvested all the potatoes in just three days this year!

We have eight milking cows, three horses, two sheep, eight
steer, many chickens and ducks.

I have lost all my teeth. The dentist wants twenty lats for new teeth. That is the one good thing about Communist times. It used to be free.

We are very worried about the coming cold. The cows are already showing thick coats. Will they produce dramatically less milk?

Thank you for the twenty lats. The neighbor who all winter long gave us water from his well when ours was too frozen to use had just asked us if we could loan him thirty-six lats so he could have his own teeth pulled. We were so worried, where would we find the money? We gave him your twenty lats!

Soon the cows will go to grass, and we hope they will produce at least ten liters more.

This is what is blooming here: apples, plums, tulips, narcissus . . .

We brought the cows that would no longer milk to the slaughterhouse, but they still have not paid what we are owed for three months.

We've picked two kilos of strawberries already and we can't pick them all. We've given the rest to the neighbors who have even less.

I am worried that there is something wrong with the bees.

*You should be careful about sending cash. There are stories
in the news about letters found slit open, whole sacks of them,
dumped in Riga's woods, undelivered, all from people in the
U.S. sending to their relatives here. Our Christmas card from
you arrived slit open. It's like the old days with the censors,
but they aren't looking for words anymore, they are looking
for dollars!*

*Milk prices are so low, because we are competing with the rest
of Europe now. We can only pray they will go up again.*

*Who will care for my bees when I am gone? No one seems
interested in learning. Will I be the last beekeeper in our
family?*

The snows this year reach to my belly.

*Remember the stand of maples that used to grow next to
Lembi? They're gone. A wicked storm knocked them down.*

The bees are dying, and we don't know why.

LIVIJA COULD NEVER decide if their words to her were like
dying bees, or downed maples, or soft milkers, or new-old
Fords the color of violets. She wanted so much *to feel along
with them*, but there was only so much that she could intuit
from these accidental-on-purpose tone poems that they composed for one another, first through the worst of the Cold War,
then through the Singing Revolution, then finally through the

collapse of the Soviet Union, and the country's early days of independence.

Dream moved faster than paper. Again and again, correspondence was lost, whether through theft, knifed-open cards left to rot in the forests outside Riga, or through silly error, additional stutters to their already elliptical communication.

You still have not said whether you received our last letter? Maybe it never came? Could you put a date on the letters you write to me, that way I can track how long it takes for your letters to reach me, and I will know when to worry if I have not heard from you for some time.

Written confirmation of her mother's death reached my grandmother long after her mother's spirit had visited her in her sleep.

The dream of the farm returning to the family had also arrived long before the envelope that my grandmother finally opened at the kitchen table where she and my grandfather had just a few years before taken turns tapping out their demands for the end to Latvia's occupation on my grandfather's typewriter.

You should know that Lembi is in ruins, her brother wrote, *but there might be a chance to get it back.*

The new government, postindependence, was willing to restore any parcel of private land confiscated under Soviet rule, so long as the former owners could document their clear claim to it.

And even before she read her brother's next words, she knew what he was about to say.

Had she not spent years imagining it into existence?

———

LET US imagine it, too: that one day, not long after the family had been exiled to Siberia, an old school friend of my grandmother happened to be wandering the local market in Gulbene. As she drifted between the vendors, she spotted an old wardrobe for sale, the wood the color of spun honey. Perhaps she ran her hands down each side, testing the ease of the grain. Or she tapped the back, to see if the maker chose flimsy boards for the places no one else would see. She tried the doors, checked the resistance of the pulls, listened for the wheeze of the hinges as they opened. It was then that she saw something on the top shelf, something pushed to a far corner, nearly out of sight.

Balanced on the tips of her milking boots, she could only just bat the edge of it with her fingertips, like a cat at work on a skein of yarn.

When it dropped in her hands she could see it was a tin, secured with a single battered clasp.

Inside, depending on who is telling the story, or who is imagining the story, maybe there was a stack of photographs, face side down.

And so the woman turned the stack over, as if preparing for a game of cards.

The first image revealed was of a face. Old and anonymous— a stout, rippled-skinned auntie, face like a hazelnut peeled from its shell. Or, maybe, a whiskery, horse-nosed uncle.

The next image was also of a face, but this one she recognized: her old school friend, lost to the war.

It seemed such an odd, impossible coincidence and so, she began to flip through the entire stack to make sure she was not imagining things.

But there she was again, her friend, now in communion dress. There were her siblings, her mother and father. There was a picture of their high school class, standing outside the baron's castle—and there, in the back, the man who would become her husband. There was a picture of the rook-haired baby girl they would have together, the child rooting about with a stick in what looked like the cabbage fields of Lembi. And there was a picture of the boy her friend once loved, before his foot found the nail.

But more important than the photographs: a tin, containing a sheet of parchment yellowing at the edges. It appeared to be some sort of document.

Among the villagers it was an open secret who had been sent away on the trains to the east, those whose farms had been seized and were never expected to come back. She knew then that this had to be the family's wardrobe, likely carried out of Lembi on someone's back while they were being loaded into the train cars at the village station.

She snapped the lid of the tin shut.

How much for this wardrobe? she said.

And then she paid the seller exactly what he asked, because she wanted to get away as fast as she could from the circumstances that led to its sale in the village market.

She kept the wardrobe in a corner of her house, and the tin upon its shelf.

The dust it gathered represented so many contingencies: *if* the family survived, *if* they ever came back to Gulbene, *if* she was still alive when they returned.

The dust tasted like the passing years, bits of hair, particles of skin, molecules of worry, specks of joy.

Old barley fields gave way to new soaring apartment blocks.

The villagers ironed their children's Young Pioneer uniforms and learned what was best said outside their children's earshot, so that the children, later, did not, in all innocence, accidentally denounce their parents to the teacher or the neighbors. They parked tractors and combines in what was once the former ballroom of the baron who sold Lembi all those years ago to his servant and shoemaker. They learned to anticipate which days the stores might put out some of the special rationed commodities—everyone could still remember the taste of the little sausages, in particular, stuffed so tightly in their casings like the weary calves of the wool-socked women who tied on their head scarves, as if preparing for battle, and committed themselves to days in line, for the momentary distraction of those little sausages, or the occasional tongue-burst of soft-whipped ice cream, the toothy spray of an orange slice in winter.

With all these new ways of living still to learn, the woman forgot about the tin in her closet.

And then, the family gave her cause to remember, stepping back as they did onto the platform of the very same train station from which they had been taken eight years earlier.

She returned the wardrobe with its tin. And with riven hands, they unclasped its crypted artifacts, let the parchment uncurl and speak.

It was the original deed to Lembi, the only record of the shoemaker's marks, the baron's loan and the recorder's sketch of the shape of the land that once was theirs, the ghostly outlines of all the swells and forests that fell within its boundaries.

As a document, it no longer held any real power, they knew, the line of "X"s made all those years ago by the shoemaker's hands now covered over by new marks: the cloven hooves and mucketed treads of the collective's cows and all the workers who cared for them, who lived in the house, too, among their herd, trailing after them, scratching at flea bites, dreading already the call for morning milking that pulled them from their beds on the floors of what was once the old kitchen, the sitting room, the old shed where milk was once left to cool.

In those strange days, when people rarely ever said exactly what they meant, at least in public, they all began to learn that lying could be a kind of truth. And when truth can be lies, and lies can be truth, then certainty is destabilized, but so is uncertainty.

Don't believe them even when they are lying, went one saying.

In other words, everything requires translation.

Truth. Lies. Lie-truths. But also, truth-lies.

To successfully anticipate the correct sequence of truth-lie-lie-truth-lie required a kind of detachment that sometimes made them doubt their own minds. Did the dog wag his tail because he was pleased to see you, or because he wanted you to think he was pleased, so that you could then realize you had in fact not pleased him at all by leaving him all day without so much as knob of gristle? Did the brigade captain who said that you had milked more than anyone else this month really mean that you had done this, or did she intend for you to realize that because she'd said you'd done a good job, you should know you'd in fact done a terrible job, that you had all done a terrible job, that the cows were going dry, but that she would be doctoring the collective farm's numbers to convince the central agricultural committee that they were surpassing their utterly unrealistic and unmeetable projections?

It was not as if anyone said, Lembi is no longer yours. You can never go back. It was simply assumed, when the family returned, that everyone would go on acting as if nothing had happened, as if things had always been this way, cows in the kitchen, ten workers to a room, your furniture in someone else's house, your laundry on another woman's line, your horse dragging someone else's plow, your hives in someone else's meadow. Sometimes, you just needed to hold a piece of paper in your hand that said, Yes, you could trust your own mind. Lembi was real for you. Its borders were real. What had happened inside those borders, that was an altogether different matter, open to interpretation and even misunderstanding. But the parchment could reassure them of this much, at least: they were not wrong to claim that their memories, good and bad, remembered and forgotten, shared and disputed, could be traced back to a specific place in the physical world. And so they kept it, this small quiet verification of a private fact, which they assumed would only ever matter to them.

To harbor it felt like a form of silent resistance, an assertion even, if only to themselves, that they still had secrets, something that belonged only to them; one small aspect of their life to which no one else had access, something they could keep separate, set apart, concealed in a battered tin—hidden evidence of what they had once possessed and lost, which meant that it possessed them still. Maybe, they decided, this was the safest form of possession in the end, harbored as they were inside a sustained and uninterrupted longing for something that was already gone. At least this way, what they had could never be taken away from them again.

So in the months after independence was declared, when there began to be talk of returning seized property, and they looked again upon the parchment locked in the tin in this new light, it is hard not to suspect that any initial excitement they would have felt at the possibility of Lembi's return might also have been accompanied by a small pulse of fear, an instinctive twitch to run and spare oneself the pain of a reunion that brought with it the possibility of new loss.

There was a certain safety to staying exactly where they were, fixed in memory, reassured of the legitimacy of their claims, certain of the wrong that had been visited upon them, never challenged by the disappointments of reality.

My grandmother wrote:

We marvel that of my childhood home something still stands. And although it pains me to hear that it is so overgrown, that you can't even see the old apple orchard anymore and that all the maples next to the house are gone, the farm can be rebuilt, and we will help you rebuild, if this is what you want. I will help you do this from afar for as long as Emils and I are able, as long as we are still breathing. We will give you all the support you need. I have such fond memories of my childhood on the farm, I would love for Lembi to return to our family, for others to experience it as I did. Wouldn't it be wonderful, brother, if you could spend your last days there, in the home where you were born, and I was born, and Ausma was born?

IN THE END, it was Ligita and Aivars who offered to try to return the farm to its former state.

If administrative order was what had ultimately banished the family, it now offered their means of return. There was no human drama, no open conflict. Only a series of mundane bureaucratic steps. Copy. Assemble. Swear. Sign. Once the original deed had been presented, there was nothing to argue. The cows left the house, the people left the barn.

Ligita and Aivars swept the rooms of manure and trash, bleached the walls of their methane stains, scrubbed through layers of unwashed funk and exhaustion and fitful night breath. They painted and papered and polished, and the fleas crabbed and pinched in tonguing waves, until their skin began to leap on its own, already anticipating the bristling touch of their legs.

With the land itself, they were forced to start over again, to level the burls of brambles and strangling grasses, to replow and reseed. They resurrected the old apple orchard but could not reclaim the original stands of gooseberries and currants. Evidence of the vines of hops that once supplied Ligita's grandfather with the ingredients for his homebrew had long since vanished. Here and there, the serrated leaves of the descendants of the old hemp crops tipped and waved above the weeds.

They filled the barn with milk cows, sheep and hogs. When the Roma came riding through, selling horses, Aivars picked out a gelding, feeling his legs for soundness, quietly assessing his disposition. They found dogs that knew in their blood how to cut a herd, how to bite without teeth. And they returned bees to hives in the meadows, so that when it was time, Janis could collect their combs, then crutch to the kitchen, where they had placed a honey extractor for him to use.

First, he would place the combs inside a basket, then he would lower the basket into the extractor's drum, which he would spin as quickly as his hands could turn the crank, trying to create enough force to fling the honey from its cells. Then he would drain the nectar that had collected in the drum's bottom into old jars.

For days after, as they walked through each scoured room, they could still smell the traces of crushed grass, new clover, fermented blackberry, the waxen peal of pollen as it is released, the sticky heat of bee's wings.

It was as if they had stitched traces of the old farm into the existing world. And it worked for a time, this reclaiming of what had been as a way to live yourself into what could be. But gradually, the patching between past and present began to show, then strain.

Aivars, who had always been active in the country's national guard, began to climb within its ranks. And while this development brought more opportunity and more pay, it also meant more travel, which frequently kept him away from home for days. All too often, that left Ligita to tend to the farm and the children on her own.

I'm worried about Ligita's health, Ausma wrote her sister, and she did not say this in her letter, but watching her daughter, she must have been reminded of her younger self, the fear and the stress she felt when the task of running Lembi fell to her alone.

My sweet Ligita's not sleeping. There's so much work to be done and she can't keep up, even as she's giving it all her strength. I'm worried she will exhaust herself to the point where she won't be able to go on.

Here was the truth: the farm was an old dream from which the new country had awakened. Without the money for machinery, for rapid expansion, without the ability to farm several hundred acres at once, a person would never be able to scratch out anything more than the most basic existence as a farmer in Latvia's new-old countryside.

Sometimes, the ending, the resolution that strikes you as so right, so happy, so perfect as to have been scripted—lost farm returned to the family from which it was taken, continuity restored, guilt assuaged, collective memories repaired—turns out to be the one you didn't really want, or need.

Was it not better to sell what they could, while they still could, to set aside whatever money they might make to help their children to go to college, to learn to use something other than their hands, to move forward without debt? Could they not hold jobs in the village, but still make time, in their off-hours, for the old ways, the smell of honey, the swing of the scythe?

Then why did they still feel so guilty to think of Lembi, abandoned, decaying, returning to ground? As far as Ausma is concerned, there was only ever one choice, and that was to let go of Lembi, to release it, once and for all.

Earth is earth, she tells me. It does not matter whether you live upon it for it to remember you, and for you to remember it.

After living through the family's first desperate attempts to hold on to the farm, never realizing just how much that would cost them—because what if she had not tried, at sixteen, to hold everything together following her father's death, what if she had said, Enough, I am too young, and they had lost Lembi then, would it really have been so bad, because how could they have sent them to Siberia when they had no more hectares to their name?—Ausma was clear: there was nothing sacred or noble about choosing home-ground above all else.

Still, she says, whenever she dreams of a house, her mind always returns her to Lembi.

It is the only home I ever visit in my dreams, she says. Even if it's not supposed to be Lembi, it always looks exactly like Lembi.

Once, I asked Ausma if she knew how Lembi got its name, and what its significance might be, but she said she didn't know.

I was too young to care about such things, she said, and I never thought to ask the people who would know while I still could.

Over the last few years, I have tried, without much luck, to come up with a satisfactory answer. Something to do with lambs, someone suggested. The baron was infatuated with Italian things, and it was a reference to something Italian that was modified over the years, someone else said. But then recently, as I was thinking about all this, about Lembi, about the difference between what we lose and what we let go, I stumbled upon a paper tracing the *anthroponymic evolution of Latvian names*.

Among the examples listed is the name *Lembe*, which is referenced in *The Chronicle of Henry of Livonia*, and thought perhaps to trace its lineage back to ancient Finno-Ugric roots.

It means love.

XX

THEY ARE too old to hay, but every morning I wake to find Ausma and Harijs at the kitchen window, scanning the road for combines, consulting the clouds, debating with each other as if they were in charge of all the surrounding fields.

The neighbor, why is he waiting so long to gather the windrows? Ausma says. Can't he see it's going to rain? He should be out there!

And then Aivars and Ligita call. Their hay is ready, and they have enough to spare. Could Ausma and Harijs use some? Ausma bites back tears. They have spent the last of their pension checks for the month, and there is still a week left before the next ones come, and they have been worrying how they will feed the horse, but they didn't want to ask for help. Oh yes, she says, and hangs up, only to realize there is a new problem. How to get the hay—and store it in the barn before the rain they are predicting arrives? Usually, another relative with a truck spares Harijs the bother of hay collection, but he is unavailable.

We are old but not helpless, Ausma says at last, as they debate what to do. Take the old wagon! Inara can help.

In Communist times, Harijs had worked training all the collective's horses. At one point, he and Ausma had cared for more than two hundred. It is immediately clear, by the speed with which he tacks the horse and hitches it to the wagon, that he has missed this part of his history, and is eager to exercise his skills as a horseman one more time.

I watch as he leans in and whispers something in the horse's ear.

What did you tell him? I ask. Harijs doesn't respond. And I can't be sure if it is because he does not hear me or because he is choosing not to answer, whether these are the kind of words that are more than words.

Holding the reins in one hand, Harijs sits on the wagon's edge, one leg dangling off the side, just above the ground. I sit behind him in the empty bed of the wagon on an old rag rug Ausma has laid for me to sit on—*to make your chariot ride a little softer*—and I keep my hands around the pitchforks to stop their rattling.

We ride in silence, Harijs concentrating on the horse's path, alert for the sound of cars. Occasionally, he will click or whistle, and the horse will adjust to his commands, but mostly it seems that Harijs communicates only with the slightest change in the tension in his body, a twitch, a small tug, nothing I can see.

Just past the crossroads pine, he maneuvers the horse toward the center of the road so that we can make room for two young women walking along the shoulder.

As they register the clatter of hooves, not the hum of tires, they stop and gape.

I've only ever seen this in books, one says.

Are you real? asks the other.

It's like a painting, says the first woman.

Would you like a ride? says Harijs.

Yes, they shout.

Harijs blushes.

The horse takes this moment to let out a stream of urine.

I can't wait to tell everyone that I have hitchhiked on a wagon, says the first woman.

When I tell Ausma the story later, about Harijs picking up young women with his wagon, she laughs. They must have been really young to be so impressed! In Communist times, well into the sixties, most people here couldn't afford cars. We still did everything with horses. Or we rode bicycles. I remember when Harijs finally saved up enough to have a motorcycle. With a sidecar! That's where I would ride. Now that was fun.

At Ligita and Aivars's house, we ease the wagon out to the back field, where they have forked the windrows into dense, towering piles.

Aren't those beautiful, says Harijs. It's almost a shame to take something so beautiful apart.

But this is what they do, peeling sheets of hay from the mound with the tines of the pitchforks, carefully spreading layer upon layer on the wagon's bed. Every so often, Ligita will hoist herself onto the growing pile and walk from one end of the wagon to the other, balancing the load, packing it down. Soon the stack of hay towers more than fifteen feet above the ground.

And this is how we ride back, perched on the very top, nothing to hold the hay in place, no rope, no straps, only the simple eloquent construction of each careful layer.

You're awake, Ausma says, as I pad into the kitchen, and tap the side of the kettle with my palm to gauge whether it's warm enough for tea.

You are here, I tell myself. You are here. You are here with Ausma, in her kitchen, with the radio playing Latvian pop songs, and there are chamomile flowers and nettle leaves drying on the stove, and there is the newspaper with its jokes, and there, through the window, is where Ausma and Harijs were married, and a little farther still, there is Ausma's birch tree.

Last night, I dreamed of a wolf in a cage. Actually, the wolf was inside a cage that had been nested inside another cage. The wolf sat with its back to me, and I could see that its pelt was lashed, laced with dozens of old wounds that had left raised scars. From somewhere behind me a voice called out: Don't look at it.

Why not? I asked.

Because some things are too dangerous even to look at, the voice said.

How did you catch it then? I asked.

It put itself inside the cage, the voice said.

At this, the wolf slowly turned its head and looked directly at me.

It had my eyes.

This morning we've already had quite the excitement, Ausma says. Her voice is clipped, cantering. Our horse is loose! Harijs went to the barn to feed him and he was gone. Now Harijs is off in his car, trying to find him, and Ligita and Aivars are looking, too.

I picture Harijs swerving down the road we just traveled with the wagon, the car stuck in second gear, his window down, neck craned for some sign of the gelding.

I tell Ausma I can run the length of what was once the old war road to check whether the horse has found its way into any of the fields that border its route. She agrees, and before I can even suggest it, she offers to tie up the dog.

The road is sun-buckled, beaten bare by the heat, and it's a long time before I can feel myself falling into an easy rhythm.

I try to focus on the drone of the barley fields, still not quite ready for harvest, but everything pointing toward fall, the cattail heads cottoning, the scouting trill of the little dog that will rush to the edge of his farm to prance and shake his beard at me, but never chase me. And now the unfalling walls of the old stone barn left to decide for itself when it is ready to give up.

I know the horse likes oak trees, prefers the scratch of their bark on his flank, and I let myself imagine briefly that I might see him in the grove coming up on my right, currycombing himself against the biggest trunks. But once I am close enough to get a better look, I can see no sign of him.

The land here dips and flattens so that I can peer far into the distance. There's nothing moving, just a faint pluming of dust. Most likely from a cow, spooked by the wind, hooves tearing at the dry hide of the fields.

I realize that I am now close to the small cottage where my grandmother's brother finally settled after his release from Siberia, and where he would have reconciled himself to the news that he could not return to Lembi to live out the last of his days when it was finally sold for good. And where I imagine, in just a few weeks, as summer gives way fully to fall, and it's time for the dead to return home again, he might just come walking, the hem of his good leg burred with the meadow's seeds, one hand on his crutch, the other at his face, swiping at the last of the mosquitoes that rise from the water that collects in a depression that rings the property like a moat, and from which the house takes its name, Gravisi, the Latvian word for *ditch*.

The only difference between the word *ditch* and a word for *grave* in Latvian, as in a carving out, an excavation, a deep impression, is the pronunciation of a single small, but critical, accent, on a single vowel.

It was here, at the cottage upon the ditch, that my grandmother's brother took his last breaths.

I had been inside my great-uncle's house only once. My cousin the mail carrier, she of the exaltation of cows, thought that there might still be letters or other family papers somewhere inside the house, which has been left largely as it was the day they wrapped his body in a blanket and pulled the door to his old home softly closed.

She offered to find me the keys.

Inside, the house smelled of night soil, the steady tunneling of earthworms, years of trapped sunlight, the sharp spiking perfume of kerosene. It was decorated with only a few items of furniture: a table, and in one corner a bed, and next to that, a small nightstand with a single drawer.

As I slid it open, I was startled to find inside a soft drift of newsprint, like a nest a mouse might make. But as I began to pull the strands apart, I realized it was a series of clippings, poems, in fact, dozens of fragile lines snipped from what looked like the obituary section of the local newspaper.

The time of hardship has ended—There are no tomorrows, only the voice of the wind. And a heart that will never again know pain, or cold.

Opposite the bed, an old wardrobe that covered most of the wall. The doors rattled at my touch, and the empty hangers inside swung and chattered. There was no poetry here, only dark corners, emptied, a single plaid button-down shirt that held the form of him. I could see that the bureau's backing seemed to be coming loose, an edge of wood protruding, perhaps popped free from its nail. But when I reached inside to knock it back, I found instead something like a frame. Artwork, I realized, that had been placed backwards, picture side facing the wall.

I drew it out, so that I might get a better look. But the glass encasing the portrait was coated with such a thick layer of grime that the image was hard to read. I considered for a moment using the shirt to wipe it clean, but somehow that felt wrong, and so I rubbed the glass with my palm, until I had removed enough of the film from the glass to suggest that what was buried here might be a woman, a portrait composed of quick pencil strokes.

Gradually, the portrait's features began to come into focus. A face pushing through the dust.

My grandmother.

She was young again, maybe sixteen, her hair in thick plaits, the same age she would have been when my grandfather carved her name, Livija, in the birch tree.

I stood there with her for what felt like a very long time.

Then, before I changed my mind, I placed the portrait back inside the bureau, and closed the door as softly as I could on the little house at the edge of the ditch, which could so easily be mistaken for a grave, and stepped outside into the sound of all the fields singing, the things alive in it waking up to the night.

———

I NEVER SEE the horse. But by the time I finally make my way back to Ausma's, Harijs has at least returned with a promising lead. A man who lives a few kilometers away spotted a gelding trying to lip green apples from his trees. When he approached, it cantered off. He thought he could still see the horse off in the tree line, waiting for a chance to resume its harvest. The man has offered to throw a rope over the horse if it returns, and promises to hold him until Harijs can come back to fetch him.

But first, lunch, says Ausma. Come, sit.

She puts a plate in front of me.

Do you know how many times I should have died? Harijs asks.

I tell Ausma about my route, about passing the house at the edge of the ditch.

All these empty houses of ours, Ausma says. Such a shame.

Livija's there, I say.

What do you mean, she's there, Ausma says. And I tell her about the portrait that I deliberately left in the wardrobe. That I like to think it's still there, safe, in the dark.

Is that where you found it? Ausma asks. In the wardrobe?

I nod.

You know, that was the wardrobe from Lembi, she says. The one the woman found. The one that had the deed inside. That got us back the farm. Funny you found her there, of all places.

Harijs must sense the tears I am struggling to hold back.

Do you have the same cows in America? he asks.

Oh, now, says Ausma, setting down her knife and shuffling

over to press me to her chest. Dear one. Don't cry. We can get that portrait for you, if it means that much.

And I want to tell her that I'm not crying because I need something of my grandmother back. I'm crying because suddenly I don't. But I can't find the words. And so I decide, for once, to leave it this way, exactly as it should be—a missing space, where she will always be.

ACKNOWLEDGMENTS

A book begins with the gift of belief. Thanks to Jamie Hatten and Barry Johnson for knowing, years before I did, that this was possible, and then doing everything to make me see it, too.

My agent, Alex Jacobs, understood instinctively all that I wished for this book, and then brought such wisdom, empathy, and kindness to every stage of its becoming. My editor, Alane Mason, regarded each word with a rare and genuine concern. All writers should be so lucky to know such generosity and understanding.

Ashley Patrick was an incredible presence helping to shepherd this book through its final stages—take heart, she said. And I've not stopped saying it to myself since. Copy editors save us in hundreds of invisible and unacknowledged ways, which is why I want to write this name, and then underline it twice: Trent Duffy. I don't have enough thanks.

As a student in the University of Iowa's Nonfiction Writing Program, I was fortunate to work with brilliant teachers: Will Jennings, David Hamilton, Patricia Foster and Bonnie Sunstein all offered crucial advice and inspiration. Special thanks to Susan Lohafer, who first helped me realize the potential of this project, and to Robin Hemley, who offered such wise direction and support in its earliest and most critical stages. But most of all, thanks to John D'Agata for giving me all that I needed to see it through.

Among Iowa's incredible and inspiring community of writers, I want to acknowledge Kendra Greene, Laurel Fantauzzo, Lina Maria Ferreira Cabeza-Vanegas, Angela Pelster-Wiebe, Lucas Mann, Kristen Radtke, Chelsea Cox and Mary Helen Kennerly.

Larry Ypil, Ariel Lewiton and Kisha Schlegel—sensitive readers, extraordinary thinkers and good, good hearts—spent years listening patiently, asking all the right questions, offering the best advice, and guiding me toward breakthrough after breakthrough.

I owe so much to my father, Juris Verzemnieks, and my aunt Inese Verzemnieks for supporting me so unconditionally and for becoming such enthusiastic research assistants, tracking down personal correspondence, documents and other ephemera I had feared lost, and which proved essential to my research. When I unearthed hidden sorrows that seemed too great to bear, they offered me their solace and their care, as did Janet Ash, to whom I will always be grateful.

Thanks to the Rona Jaffe Foundation and the Stanley-UI Foundation for their generous support, which allowed me to travel to Latvia.

In Riga, Guntis Svitins of the National Archives and historian Lelde Neimane of the Occupation Museum offered invaluable assistance navigating archives and special collections related to Latvia's Siberian exiles.

Most of all, I must thank my Latvian relatives, who opened their homes and lives to me. In Riga, Janis and Lija Verzemnieks, Janis and Felicija Verzemnieks, Evita Mazure, and Iveta and Rolands Mucenieks gave me shelter and revealed the city to me. In Rezekne, Aigars and Zanna Kronitis invested hours translating the secret Siberian files on our family from Russian. I will always look back on my time in Gulbene, in particular, with such intense gratitude. And that is because of Inese Donuka, who spent hours with me in the fields, helping me to see them through new eyes, and who placed in my hands a bundle of letters written by my grandmother during the fifty years she spent in exile. Also, Aivars Kronitis, faithful chauffeur and trusted guide through the region's forests and secret ruins, and his wife, Ligita Kronite, securer of survey maps and library books, keeper of family stories and knowledge of the old folkways, all of which came to influence me profoundly.

My deepest thanks go to Harijs and Ausma Sebris, for showing me how it is possible to live so beautifully and openheartedly, despite enduring so much.

And finally, to Nick Jones—without you, I would never have found the words:

Dwi'n dy garu di.

SOURCES

Over the course of this project, I have been informed, guided, challenged, enraged and inspired by a number of sources. Below is a list of works consulted, beyond what I unearthed in archives and through interviews. While by no means exhaustive, it represents those sources that I am most indebted to for informing my decisions in how I chose to tell this story.

Applebaum, Anne. *Gulag: A History*. New York: Doubleday, 2003.

Barkahan, Menachem. *Extermination of the Jews in Latvia: 1941–1945*. Riga: Shamir, 2008.

Blécourt, Willem De. "A Journey to Hell: Reconsidering the Livonian 'Werewolf.'" *Magic, Ritual, and Witchcraft* 2, no. 1 (2008): 49–67.

Blumbergs, Andrew James. *The Nationalization of Latvians and the Issue of Serfdom: The Baltic German Literary Contribution in the 1780s and 1790s*. Amherst, N.Y.: Cambria, 2008.

Boder, David P. *Topical Autobiographies of Displaced People: Recorded Verbatim in Displaced Persons Camps with a Psychological and Anthropological Analysis*. Chicago, 1950.

Bunkše, Edmunds. "God, Thine Earth Is Burning: Nature Attitudes and the Latvian Drive for Independence." *GeoJournal* 26, no. 2 (1992): 203–9.

———. "Latvian Folkloristics." *The Journal of American Folklore* 92, no. 364 (1979): 196–214.

Displaced Persons. Hearings Before the Subcommittee on Amendments to the Displaced Persons Act of the Committee on the Judiciary, United States Senate, Eighty-first Congress, First and Second Sessions, on Bills to Amend the Displaced Persons Act of 1948. Washington, D.C: GPO, 1950.

Dribins, Leo. *Ebreji Latvija*. Riga: Elpa, 2002.

Duerr, Hans Peter. *Dreamtime: Concerning the Boundary Between Wilderness and Civilization*. Oxford: B. Blackwell, 1985.

Eksteins, Modris. *Walking Since Daybreak: A Story of Eastern Europe, World War II, and the Heart of Our Century*. Boston: Houghton Mifflin, 1999.

Ezergailis, Andrew. *The Holocaust in Latvia: 1941–1944: The Missing Center*. Riga: Historical Institute of Latvia, 1996.

Gatrell, Peter, and Nick Baron. *Warlands: Population Resettlement and State Reconstruction in the Soviet–East European Borderlands, 1945–50*. Basingstoke, Eng.: Palgrave Macmillan, 2009.

Haywood, A. J. *Siberia: A Cultural History*. Oxford: Oxford University Press, 2010.

Henricus. *The Chronicle of Henry of Livonia*, trans. James A. Brundage. Madison: University of Wisconsin Press, 1961.

Hudson, Hugh D. *Peasants, Political Police, and the Early Soviet State: Surveillance and Accommodation Under the New Economic Policy*. New York: Palgrave Macmillan, 2012.

Hulme, Kathryn. *The Wild Place*. Boston: Little, Brown, 1953.

Karasa, Diana, ed. *Latviesu Sadzives Tradicijas Un Godi*. Riga: Jumava, 2011.

Katzenelenbogen, Uriah. *The Daina; An Anthology of Lithuanian and Latvian Folk-songs*. Chicago: Lithuanian News Publishing, 1935.

Khlevniuk, O. V. *The History of the Gulag: From Collectivization to the Great Terror.* New Haven: Yale University Press, 2004.

Kovtunenko, Rolands. *Battle at More.* Riga: Timermanis and Vejins, 2009.

Lazda, Mara. "Women, Nation, and Survival: Latvian Women in Siberia 1941–1957." *Journal of Baltic Studies* 36, no. 1 (2005): 1–12.

Liva, Arvi, and Ilze Loze. "Mesolithic and Neolithic Habitation of the Eastern Baltics." *Radiocarbon* 35, no. 3 (1993): 503–6.

Lumans, Valdis O. *Latvia in World War II.* New York: Fordham University Press, 2006.

Memo to America: The DP Story: The Final Report of the U.S. Displaced Persons Commission. Washington, D.C.: GPO, 1952.

Merkel, Garlieb. *Latvieši: Sevišķi Vidzemē, Filozofiskā Gadsimteņa Beigās.* Riga: Zvaigzne ABC, 1999.

Misiunas, Rommuald. *The Baltic States: Years of Dependence, 1940–1990.* Berkeley: University of California Press, 1993.

Murray, Alan V. *The Clash of Cultures on the Medieval Baltic Frontier.* Farnham, Eng.: Ashgate, 2009.

Narkeliūnaité, Saloméja. *DP Baltic Camp at Seedorf.* Hamburg: UNRRA Team 295, 1947.

Nollendorfs, Valters, and Erwin Oberländer. *The Hidden and Forbidden History of Latvia Under Soviet and Nazi Occupations 1940–1991: Selected Research of the Commission of the Historians of Latvia.* Riga: Institute of the History of Latvia, 2005.

Petersen, Roger Dale. *Resistance and Rebellion: Lessons from Eastern Europe.* Cambridge: Cambridge University Press, 2001.

Plakans, Andrejs. *The Latvians: A Short History.* Stanford, Calif.: Hoover Institution Press/Stanford University, 1995.

Press, Bernhard. *The Murder of the Jews in Latvia: 1941–1945.* Evanston, Ill.: Northwestern University Press, 2000.

Rislakki, Jukka. *The Case for Latvia: Disinformation Campaigns Against a Small Nation: Fourteen Hard Questions and Straight Answers About a Baltic Country.* Amsterdam: Rodopi, 2008.

Rozkalne, Anita, ed. *Latvju Dainas.* Riga: Latvijas Universitates Literatures, Folkloras and Makslas Institutes, 2012.

Shephard, Ben. *The Long Road Home: The Aftermath of the Second World War.* New York: Alfred A. Knopf, 2011.

Silgailis, Arturs. *Latvian Legion.* San Jose, Calif.: R.J. Bender, 1986.

Skultans, Vieda. *The Testimony of Lives: Narrative and Memory in Post-Soviet Latvia.* London: Routledge, 1998.

———. "Theorizing Latvian Lives: The Quest for Identity." *Journal of the Royal Anthropological Institute* 3 (2001): 761–80.

Snyder, Timothy. *Bloodlands: Europe Between Hitler and Stalin.* New York: Basic, 2010.

Šteimanis, Josifs, and Edward Anders. *History of Latvian Jews.* Boulder, Col.: East European Monographs, 2002.

Vikis-Freibergs, Vaira. "Linear and Cyclic Time in Traditional and Modern Latvian Poetry." *Board of Regents of the University of Oklahoma* 51, no. 4 (1977): 538–43.

———. "Sink or Swim: On Associative Structure in Longer Latvian Folk Songs." *Oral Tradition* (1997): 279–307.

Vilka, Inta. *Caur Sirdi Plustosa Dzive.* Riga: Vesta-LK, 2013.

Viola, Lynne. "The Aesthetic of Stalinist Planning and the World of the Special Villages." *Kritika: Explorations in Russian and Eurasian History* 4, no. 1 (2003): 101–28.

———. *The Unknown Gulag: The Lost World of Stalin's Special Settlements.* Oxford: Oxford University Press, 2007.

Wyman, Mark. *DP: Europe's Displaced Persons, 1945–1951.* Ithaca, N.Y.: Cornell University Press, 1989.

Zelčs, Vitalys, and Māris Nartišs, eds. "Late Quaternary Terrestrial Processes, Sediments, and History: From Glacial to Postglacial Environments." University of Latvia, 2014; available at www.geovip.lu.lv/fileadmin/user_upload/lu_portal/projekti/geovip/konferences/Peribaltic_2014_Latvia_Excursion_Guide_and_Abstract_book.pdf.